PRINCETON MONOGRAPHS

IN ART AND ARCHAEOLOGY

XXXVIII

PUBLISHED FOR THE

DEPARTMENT OF ART AND ARCHAEOLOGY

PRINCETON UNIVERSITY

Joachim Patinir

BY ROBERT A. KOCH

PRINCETON UNIVERSITY PRESS · 1968

PRINCETON, NEW JERSEY

JOACHIM PATINIR

TO THE MEMORY
OF A GREAT TEACHER
AND DEAR FRIEND,

Clemens Sommer

PREFACE

JOACHIM PATINIR has always been acknowledged as the first artist in the Low Countries to make an autonomous subject of landscape painting, notwithstanding the fact that the time in which he lived, the first quarter of the sixteenth century, still demanded that the picture contain a religious theme. His singular accomplishment was recognized even in his own lifetime by no less eminent an authority than Albrecht Dürer, who became a friend of Patinir in Antwerp during his trip to the Netherlands. Apart from his historical importance, Patinir was a "good landscape painter" (Dürer), and his works were avidly acquired by royal as well as by affluent bourgeois collectors.

This is the first monograph on the artist. In it I have attempted to assemble all of the known facts about Patinir and his paintings, together with as many scholarly opinions as seemed of value. The bibliography is not large, and in fact there have been only two comparatively comprehensive studies of the style of Patinir's landscape painting. The earlier was by Ludwig Baldass in 1918, in the Vienna *Jahrbuch*. This was a pioneering article, astonishingly prophetic and still superb, on the development of landscape painting in the Netherlands from Patinir to Bruegel. The second study was by M. J. Friedländer in 1931, in the ninth volume of his monumental *Altniederländische Malerei*. Although he largely ignored Baldass' successful attempt to define the true style of Patinir and thus to form the basis for a separation of his paintings from the many that were created in imitation of it, Friedländer compiled the first catalogue of the paintings; and it has remained the only one to date. His list contains many incorrect attributions, and many of these have continued to pass as "Patinir" to the present day. In fact, there are many paintings in museums, private collections, and in the art market which are called "Patinir"—often with qualification—for want of another name. This is as much a tribute to his stature as it is a manifestation of the confusion and ignorance of art historians on the matter. Since Friedländer's catalogue was compiled a quarter of a century ago, several paintings have come to light, many have changed ownership, and a number have "disappeared" in the trade and in private collections. I have devoted a separate chapter to the Master of the Half-Lengths as landscape painter, for he was a very close follower, and the only identifiable one, of the style and iconography of Patinir. Baldass, in the article mentioned above, first pointed the way to an understanding of this anonymous Master as a landscape painter. Following this scholar's lead, I have been able to attribute to the Master of the Half-Lengths many additional paintings, including very fine ones which until now have passed as works by Patinir. A number of paintings are reproduced for the first time.

Of paramount importance for my research have been the photographic archives

of the Platt Collection of Princeton University, the Frick Art Reference Library, the Witt Library of the Courtauld Institute of Art, and, most important of all, the Netherlands Institute for Art History (the *R.K.D.*) in The Hague, which contains the collection of photographs that belonged to M. J. Friedländer, in addition to its own unparalleled assemblage of photographs of paintings by the Dutch and Flemish schools. Each institution had one or more photographs that the others did not. The custodians of all of these collections were very cooperative, it is a pleasure to report. I have also benefited from information and opinions furnished by many art historians, museum directors and curators, owners of pictures and dealers. Among these I should like to single out for special thanks Mr. Martin Davies, Professor Jan Białostocki, Professor Wolfgang Stechow, Professor Julius Held, Dr. H. Pauwels, Dr. Hans Haug, Professor L. V. Randall, Professor H. Gerson, Dr. Jan Lauts, Mr. M. de Pret; and Professors Jonathan Brown, David Coffin, and Felton Gibbons, colleagues at Princeton University. Others who have made important contributions include Professor Herbert Kessler, Professor Sadja Herzog, Dr. Evan Turner, Miss Barbara Sweeny, Professor Colin Eisler, Professor J. R. Judson, and Messrs. Robert Draper, David Farmer, Charles Stanford, and Charles Millard. The text has been enriched by a number of pertinent observations, chiefly iconographical, that were made by graduate students at Princeton in a seminar on Patinir that I conducted in the Spring of 1965: Paul Richelson, Oliver Banks, Archer St.-Clair, George Goldner, and in particular Glenn Andres.

The book was made possible through generous grants for photographs from the Margaret and Millard Meiss Fund, and for travel from the Spears Fund, both of the Department of Art and Archaeology, Princeton University. Craig Harbison has been an invaluable assistant.

I am greatly indebted to Princeton University Press, especially to Miss Harriet Anderson for her careful and discerning transformation of my manuscript into this book and to P. J. Conkwright for its handsome design.

Princeton, N.J.   ROBERT A. KOCH
23 November 1966

CONTENTS

PHOTOGRAPHIC SOURCES

A. C. L., Brussels, Figs. 4, 5, 10, 34, 58, 69
Alinari, Florence, Figs. 14, 15
Anderson, Rome, Figs. 28, 39, 44, 45, 49, 54
Archives Photographiques, Paris, Fig. 26
Ashmolean Museum, University of Oxford, Fig. 3
Bearsted Coll., Banbury, National Trust, Fig. 66
Berlin-Dahlem, Museum, Figs. 33, 40, 92
Boymans-Van Beuningen Museum, Rotterdam, Figs. 2, 13
Foto Mas, Barcelona, Figs. 41, 42, 43, 46, 47, 50, 51, 52, 56, 71
Gabinetto Fotografico Nazionale, Rome, Fig. 36
Galerie Thyssen, Lugano, Fig. 12
John G. Johnson Coll., Philadelphia, Figs. 20, 22, 23, 24, 25, 60, 74
Kress Collection, National Gallery of Art, Washington, D.C., Fig. 68
Kunsthaus, Zurich, Figs. 32, 75, 76
Kunsthistorisches Museum, Vienna, Figs. 6, 7, 8, 9, 79, 80
L. V. Randall, Montreal, Fig. 86
M. Abel-Menne, Wuppertal-Elberfeld, Fig. 31
Metropolitan Museum of Art, New York, Frontispiece, Figs. 35, 37, 38
Minneapolis Institute of Arts, Fig. 21
Musée de Dijon, Figs. 59, 84
National Gallery, London, Figs. 30, 57, 73, 88
Nationalmuseum, Stockholm, Fig. 62
North Carolina Museum of Art, Raleigh, Figs. 81, 82
Öffentliche Kunstsammlung, Basel, Fig. 91
Paul Bijtebier, Brussels, Fig. 90
Philadelphia Museum of Art, Fig. 11
R. K. D., The Hague, Figs. 16, 17, 18, 64, 67, 72
Staatliche Kunsthalle, Karlsruhe, Fig. 1
Statens Museum For Kunst, Copenhagen, Fig. 87
University Museum, Uppsala, Fig. 83
Wildenstein & Co., New York, Fig. 65
William Rockhill Nelson Gallery of Art, Kansas City, Figs. 77, 78

ILLUSTRATIONS

XV

JOACHIM PATINIR

CHAPTER ONE

PATINIR AND HIS PATRONS

ALBRECHT DÜRER'S diary of his journey to the Netherlands during the years 1520-1521 is a well-known mine of interesting observations and has proved to be our richest contemporary source of information about Joachim Patinir.[1] Dürer met many prominent artists in the great port city of Antwerp, including the visiting Hollander, Lucas van Leyden; but his strongest affinity was to Patinir, as attested by a number of recurrent references in the diary. As though Dürer sensed Patinir's position in history as the first painter to specialize in landscape painting, he characterized his new friend as "the good landscape painter" ("der gut landschafft mahler")—the first time the word landscape in this context is recorded in German literature.[2]

In scattered references we are given the following information about Patinir in the diary.[3] In August 1520, Dürer invited him to dinner; and on two other occasions he invited Patinir's apprentice (*knecht*). He reimbursed with his own graphic works both Master, for the loan of his colors, and apprentice, for services rendered. From March 1521 until his departure from the Low Countries in July, Dürer was invited to the festivities preceding and following the second marriage of Patinir. This was evidently a splendid affair at which two plays were performed, the first of which was "especially pious and devout." Three weeks or so before the wedding, Dürer had drawn the likeness of Patinir, "and made him besides another likeness."[4] Dürer also presented Patinir with "Hans Grün's work," presumably prints;[5] and

---

[1] J. Veth and S. Muller, *Albrecht Dürers niederländische Reise*, II, Berlin, 1918, pp. 211ff. (on Dürer's relationship with Patinir). The diary has been newly edited by H. Rupprich, *Dürer Schriftlicher Nachlass*, I, Berlin, 1956.

[2] Rupprich, p. 195, n. 596. Gombrich reminds us that it was not in Antwerp but in Venice that the word landscape is first applied to an individual painting. In the very same year, 1521, Marc Antonio Michiel noted "molte tavolette de paesi" in the collection of Cardinal Grimani (and these were very likely Netherlandish pictures). E. Gombrich, "Renaissance Artistic Theory and the Development of Landscape Painting," *G. d.B.-A.*, Ser. 6, Vol. 41, 1953, p. 339.

[3] Rupprich, *op.cit.*, gives the German text on the following pages: p. 152, lines 87-89, 92-96; p. 167, lines 266-69; p. 169, lines 24-26 (5 May 1521) 59-63; p. 172 (19-20 May 1521) lines 8-10 ("Den maister Joachim hab ich 4 Christophel auff graw papir verhöcht."); p. 175, lines 76-77 ("Ich hab meister Joachim des Grünhanssen ding geschenckt.")

[4] It is not clear whether both drawings were portraits of Patinir, but most critics have assumed so. An exception is the romantic view of M. Conway, who guesses that the second "likeness" was that of the lady "so soon to be his bride" (*The Van Eycks and their Followers*, 1921, p. 349). The original drawings have disappeared. On portraits of Patinir see Wurzbach, 1910, p. 310. The Weimar drawing has since been rejected as a likeness of Patinir.

[5] That the "work" was a *painting* by Hans Baldung Grien, which seems unlikely, has been stated by a number of critics, including J. Hel-

he made for him a drawing, or drawings, on gray paper of "four Christophers." Of Patinir's own work, Dürer was given a small panel depicting Lot and his Daughters, presented to him by Adrian Herbouts, advocate to the Council of Antwerp. The departure of the famed Master of Nuremberg from the Netherlands occasioned the following revealing, and poignant, remark in the diary: "In all my doings, spendings, sales and other dealings, in all my connections with high and low, I have suffered loss in the Netherlands; and Lady Margaret [the Governess Margaret of Austria] in particular gave me nothing for what I made and presented to her."[6]

To Dürer's important contribution to our knowledge of the biography of Joachim Patinir official Antwerp records add but little. The "Liggeren" of the painters' guild record that in the year 1515 there was received as "meester" "Jochim Patenier, scildere," at the same time as the eminent Gerard David, temporarily enrolled from Bruges ("Meester Gheraet van Brugghe, scildere").[7] Although documentation has not survived, it is likely that both participated as master decorators in that year for the joyous entry into Antwerp of the Archduke Charles. We learn nothing more of Patinir's career as a painter in the lists of the guild; he did not become dean nor, apparently, did he officially enroll a pupil.

Other city records give a certain amount of additional information, all of which pertains to the vital statistics of his life as a citizen of Antwerp. With his first wife, Francisca Buyst, daughter of the painter Eduard Buyst from Dendermonde, Patinir bought a house on March 31, 1520.[8] That he remarried on May 5, 1521, we learn from Dürer's diary; and the city records infer that he died before October 5, 1524, when the sale of the house named Johanna Noyts as widow. His three children were daughters—Brigitta and Anna by his first wife, and Petronella by his second. Among the guardians of the first two children was Quentin Massys.[9]

---

big, "Joachim Patenier," *Revue de l'art chretien*, 1900, p. 467; and Wurzbach, 1910, p. 309. I have been able to trace no stylistic or iconographic influence of Baldung's graphic works on the art of Patinir.

[6] Rupprich, *op.cit.*, pp. 175-76, lines 128-34.

[7] P. Rombouts and T. van Lerius, *Les Liggeren . . .* , I, Antwerp, 1872, p. 83.

[8] Two documents were discovered by Léon de Burbure, and their contents were published in the original Flemish by A. Pinchart in the notes to his translation of Crowe and Cavalcaselle, *Anciens peintres flamands*, I, Brussels, 1862, pp. CCLXXXIV-V, nn. 3 and 1. Pinchart's passage is repeated in the H. Hymans ed. of Van Mander, *Le Livre des peintres*, I, Paris, 1884, p. 195.

I quote the French translation by A. Michiels of the document describing the purchase of the house (*Histoire de la peinture flamande*, IV, 2d ed., Paris, 1866, p. 402, n. 1):

"Jean Wrage, verrier, et Hase Staecx, sa femme, vendent à Joachim de Patinier, peintre, et à Françoise Buyst, son épouse, une maison avec la moitié d'un jardon, qu'ils feront limiter ensemble, avec la cour, la moitié du puits, la moitié de la margelle, fundo et pertinenciis, situes en cette ville, rue Courte de l'Hôpital (corte Gasthuys-strate). . . ."

[9] The other two guardians were the painters Karel Alaerts and Patinir's brother-in-law Jan Buyst. Three different persons were named guardians for Petronella (see Michiels, *op.cit.*, pp. 404-5).

Although the portrait of Patinir that Dürer drew in Antwerp has evidently not survived, an engraving based upon it was made by Cornelis Cort and issued in the *Effigies* of the Liége humanist Dominicus Lampsonius.[10] This volume of portraits of famous painters of the Low Countries, accompanied by laudatory verses in Latin, was published in Antwerp in 1572 by the widow of Hieronymus Cock.[11] The following verse appears under the portrait of Patinir, which is entitled "Ioachimo Dionatensi Pictori" ("Joachim of Dinant, Painter"):

"If, Joachim, your image burns with an incomparable brilliance among the others, it is not only because the hand of Cort has engraved it on copper, a hand which fears no other rival. But it is also because Dürer, admiring your art, as you painted fields and houses, once drew your image on parchment; Cort, rivaling him with this drawing, has surpassed himself, and all the others as well."[12]

Dealing exclusively with the Dürer-Cort portrait (which is anything but flattering), the verse is a curious tribute to the famous landscape painter.

Modern critics have placed the birth of Patinir between about 1480 and 1490, a decision based largely upon his appearance in the Cort engraving. Difficult though it be to judge the age of a sitter from a portrait, and especially an engraved copy, Patinir appears to be a man at least in his late thirties. His year of birth must thus have been around 1485; and he died in 1524, three years after the prototype of Cort's image was drawn from life by Dürer. A comparatively early death at about the age of forty would not be incompatible with our knowledge of his career and family life, nor with the number of surviving paintings that one can attribute to him.[13]

The question of whether the Master was born at Dinant, as Lampsonius is the first to state, or at Bouvignes, as Lodovico Guicciardini had earlier remarked in his *Descrittione di tutti i paesi bassi*,[14] has been a much argued question, now a thoroughly tiresome one, of little importance. These neighboring towns situated up the river from Namur were long-standing rivals. Since Dinant was politically affiliated with Liége, and Bouvignes with Namur, it is not surprising that Lampsonius, who served

---

[10] See Rupprich, *op.cit.*, p. 195, n. 588; and Michiels, *op.cit.*, on the rather bizarre appearance of Patinir.

[11] I have used the recent critical edition by Jean Puraye, *Dominique Lampson, les Effigies des Peintres célèbres des Pays-Bas*, Desclée de Brouwer, 1956, pp. 38-39. Plate 8 of the original edition.

[12] "Has inter omnes nulla quod vivacius/ Joachime imago cernitur/ Expressa, quam vultus tui, non hinc modo./ Factum est, quod illam Curtij/ In aere Dextra incidit, alteram sibi./

Quae non timet nunc aemulan/ Sed quod tuam Durerus admirans manum/ Dum rura pingis et casas./ Olim exaravit in palimpsesto tuos./ Vultus ahena cuspide./ Quas aemulatus lineas se Curtius/ Nedum praeivit Caeteros." (The translation is mine.)

[13] M. J. Friedländer says that Patinir appears to be "at least 40" and would thus have been born ca. 1480 (IX, 1931, p. 103). L. Baldass guesses the age of "about 45" (1918, p. 119).

[14] Published in Antwerp in 1567.

5

for years as private secretary to the bishops of Liége, wished to "claim" Patinir for Dinant. The matter revolves about the question of the place of birth of Herri met de Bles. This painter of landscapes, possibly a nephew of Joachim Patinir and a follower of his style, is probably to be identified as the "Herry de Patenir" who became master in the Antwerp guild in 1535.[15] Guicciardini had written that Joachim Patinir was from Bouvignes ("Giovacchino di Pattenier di Bovines"), and Herri met de Bles from Dinant ("Henrico da Dinant").[16] It is Guicciardini's account which Vasari followed in the second edition of his *Vite* in 1568,[17] while Van Mander[18] takes the side of Lampsonius. Later writers, such as Sandrart,[19] tend to use only Van Mander as their source of information on Patinir. Lampsonius says in his verse beneath the engraved portrait of Herri met de Bles:

> "The city of Dinant gave birth to a painter praised by the painter-poet in his verse. The picturesque sites of his country made an artist of him; he was trained by no master. Envying its neighbor's glory, poor Bouvignes produced Henry, skilled in the art of landscape. But as much as Bouvignes grants this to Dinant, Joachim, Henry grants it to you."[20]

We might do well to believe Guicciardini, perhaps the more dispassionate historian since he was a Florentine who resided, after 1542, in his adopted city of Antwerp. In a chapter on Antwerp in the *Descrittione*, Guicciardini has an important account of the history of the fine arts of the Low Countries, and it is certain that he would have been acquainted if not with Herri met de Bles personally then at least with his paintings, the most fashionable style of landscape painting in Antwerp at the time. I am therefore inclined to believe that Joachim Patinir was born in "poor" Bouvignes.[21]

The surname of both painters was "Patinir" ("Patinier," "Patenier"), though the nickname "met de Bles," Van Mander tells us, was adopted for the younger painter because of the locks of white hair on his forehead.[22] Joachim spelled his name in two different ways, "Patinir" and "Patinier," on the three (and perhaps five)

---

[15] Rombouts and Lerius, *op.cit.*, p. 124; Friedländer, XIII, 1936, p. 36. That this person was not a son of Patinir is evident, since the archives mention only daughters.

[16] *Op.cit.*, p. 98.

[17] Ed. Milanesi, VII, Florence, 1881, p. 583.

[18] *Het Schilderboek*, Haerlem, 1604, fol. 219r.

[19] *Der Teutschen Academie, zweyter Theil*, Nuremberg, 1675, p. 244.

[20] Ed. Jean Puraye, *op.cit.*, pp. 50-51:
"Henrico Blesio Bovinati Pictori
Pictorem urbs dederat Dionatum Eburonia, pictor/ Quem proximis dixit poeta versibus./ Illum adeo artificem patriae situs ipse, magistro,/ Aptissimus, vix edocente fecerat./ Hanc laudem invidit vicinae exile Bovinum,/ Et rura doctum pingere Henricum dedit./ Sed quantum cedit Dionato exile Bovinum,/ Ioachime, tantum cedit Henricus tibi." (The translation is mine.)

[21] In the more recent literature Dinant seems to be preferred.

[22] Ed. H. Hymans, p. 197. The curls are to be seen in the dapper portrait of Met de Bles engraved for the *Effigies* of Lampsonius, *ed.cit.*, p. 51.

6

certain paintings by him that bear his signature.[23] On the two earliest surviving pictures, *Landscape with St. Jerome* (Karlsruhe), and *Landscape with the Flight into Egypt* (Antwerp), the spelling is "Patinir." Hulin de Loo says that this is the Walloon form of the French name "Patinier" (meaning "maker of pattens," a type of wooden shoe), and that this translates into Flemish "de Patenier."[24] Thus Patinir at first chose a spelling that conformed with his "French" background on the Meuse. Even this consistency is remarkable in an age notoriously insouciant in the matter of spelling. On the other hand the capital letter "D" that he consistently placed between his given and surname remains an intriguing puzzle. Three solutions have been suggested: *"Dionatensis"* ("of Dinant");[25] *"Dictus"* or *"Dicti"* ("called");[26] and *"de"* as a Flemish article ("the") and as the French nobiliary particle ("of").[27] None of these proposals seems to give the answer.

Van Mander apparently confused Joachim Patinir and "Herry de Patenir" (met de Bles), and this confusion has emerged now and again ever since, even in the attribution of paintings to the two masters. I should like to quote in its entirety Van Mander's account of "Joachim Patenier, Painter of Dinant," as given in his *Schilderboek* of 1604. As a characteristic biographical entry in this earliest comprehensive historical study of the art of the Low Countries, it is an interesting exercise in misinformation:

[23] Karlsruhe *Jerome*, "Opus Joachim · D · Patinir"; Antwerp *Flight*, "Opus Joachim · D · Patinir"; Vienna *Baptism*, "Opus Joachim · D · Patinier" (wrongly recorded in Wurzbach, 1910, p. 311, as "Patinir"). All of these inscriptions are informally block-printed in upper and lower case letters arranged on three lines: Opus/ Joachim D/ Patinir.

Two other paintings, both late, bear signatures (by Patinir himself?). They are written on one line, placed at the bottom of the composition: near the center in the Prado *Jerome*, "Joachim D Patinier"; and at the right in the Prado *Anthony*, "Opus Joachim *at*nier" (*Catalogo de los Cuadros, Museo del Prado*, 1952, pp. 468-69).

The *Rest on the Flight* in the Comte de Vogüé Collection, Dijon, which I feel is a splendid workshop painting (see Catalogue No. 21), bears a one-line signature, "Joachim de Patinier." This was perhaps not affixed by Patinir himself.

The *Landscape with Shepherds* (Fig. 69) in the Michel de Pret-Roose Collection, Schoten (Antwerp)—a fine painting by a follower of Patinir, in my opinion (see Catalogue No. 36)

—bears the signature Opus/ Joachim/ D Patinir on the tree trunk in the lower right-hand corner of the composition.

[24] Bruges Exh. of 1902, *Catalogue critique*, p. 121.

[25] A. Michiels, *op.cit.*, pp. 401-2; H. B. Wehle, "A Triptych by Patinir," *Bul. of the Met. Mus. of Art*, N.Y., 31, 1936, p. 82.

[26] Pinchart, *op.cit.*, *Notes*, p. cclxxxiii. This opinion was followed by A. J. Wauters, *The Flemish School of Painting*, London, 1885, p. 94.

[27] A. Michiels, *loc.cit.*; M. Davies, *Early Netherlandish School* (Cat. Nat. Gal. London), rev. ed., 1955, p. 119, does not accept "de."

Wurzbach reports a delightful fantasy, that the "Joachim D" has been read as "Joachimo" and the conclusion drawn therefrom that Patinir was in Italy (1910, p. 310; supported by Fierens-Gevaert, *Les primitifs flamands*, iii, Brussels, 1910, p. 219). Only G. J. Hoogewerff in recent times has suggested that Patinir went to Italy ("Joachim Patinir en Italie," *Revue d'art*, 45, 1928, *passim*). The popularity of Patinir's landscape paintings in Italy notwithstanding, there is no valid evidence of such a trip.

"The famous and imposing city of Antwerp, prosperous because of its commerce, attracted the most eminent artists from many parts, and in large numbers, since art flourishes where there is wealth. Among others this Joachim Patenier, who was born in Dinant, was attracted there. He became a member of the guild and noble company of painters of Antwerp in the year of our Lord 1515. He painted landscapes in a particular way, very beautiful and pure, his trees being stippled ("getippelt"). Also he included nice little figures, so that his works were in demand, were sold and carried to divers countries. It was his custom to place somewhere in his landscapes a little man answering the call of nature, whence he was called "de kakker" [the defecator]. One repeatedly looked for this little man, just as one did for the little owl of Herri met de Bles. Besides being an artist, this Patenier was someone who led a wild life and was very prone to drink, so that he would waste entire days at the inn spending his money until the need for more took him back to his profitable brushes. An apprentice Frans Mostert, whom he often threw into the street when he was difficult and drunken, had to suffer a lot despite his wish to learn the trade. Albrecht Dürer, when he was in Antwerp, was a great admirer of Patenier's art, and made a very handsome portrait of him with a copper needle on a slate, or perhaps on a little metal plate. One sees very pretty landscapes by Patenier in various collections. In Middleburg, at the house of Melchior Wijntgis, mint master of Zeeland, one finds three remarkable works by him, of which one, full of small figures, represents a battle, so well and finely treated that no miniature could surpass it." (The account ends with a quotation of the verse of Lampsonius.)[28]

In the *errata* at the end of the first edition, Van Mander wrongly "corrects" the year of Joachim's entry into the guild, which took place in 1515, to 1535. Since 1535 is the year in which "Herry de Patenier" (met de Bles) was enrolled in the guild, it is possible that some of his remarks about Joachim might refer instead to Herri.[29] There is, of course, neither evidence nor proof that either artist was debauched; and it is not very likely that Frans Mostaert would have been a pupil of Joachim Patinir, since he himself is recorded as enrolling a pupil in the Antwerp guild in 1553, twenty-

[28] My translation is based upon the first ed. of *Het Schilderboek*, Haerlem, 1604, fol. 219r, and upon the modern Dutch edition, which follows the second edition in 1618, *Het Schilder-Boek van Carel van Mander*, 3rd printing, Amsterdam, 1946, p. 68.

Van Mander once again refers to Patinir in the *Schilderboek*. In his account of Joos van Cleve is the remark, "Melchior Wijntgis owns a very pretty Maria, for which Joachim Patenier painted an especially fine landscape." (Mod. Dutch ed., p. 83.)

[29] This opinion was already voiced in 1862 by Pinchart, *op.cit.*, p. CCLXXXV (quoted in Hymans, *op.cit.*, p. 195).

nine years after Joachim's death.[30] Frans Mostaert, on the other hand, is also reported by Van Mander to have been a pupil of Herri met de Bles, which may well have been true.[31] One must also question Van Mander's observation, induced no doubt by the desire to titillate his readers, that Patinir customarily included the figure of a little man answering the call of nature, like the little owl in paintings by Met de Bles. Whereas an owl does occur in works by Bles, so frequently in fact that the painter was called *Civetta* in Italy, where his pictures were eagerly collected, the *kakker* is very rare in paintings by Patinir. In the Prado *Rest on the Flight* a tiny male figure squats beside a distant farmhouse; while another appears to be relieving himself in the hell of the *Landscape with Charon's Boat* (Prado). However, Van Mander could have known neither of these pictures, for they were already in the collection of the Emperor in Spain.[32] On the other hand we can believe Van Mander's remark that Patinir's paintings "were in demand, were sold and carried to divers countries." Landscape paintings would have appealed to worldly travelers of every sort, especially merchants or merchant-bankers, who comprised a newly expanded clientele in the early sixteenth century. Bourgeois collectors wanted paintings that were not only pleasant to look at but mobile and negotiable, and Patinir's sanctified landscape adventures nicely fulfilled these requirements. Antwerp became the leading center of commerce in all of Northern Europe after 1516, when merchants from Portugal and Southern Germany, and in fact from everywhere but Spain, removed from Bruges to the deep-water port city on the Scheldt.[33] "Art flourishes where there is wealth," Van Mander explained, and to meet the demand in Antwerp artists came in ever-growing numbers from all over the Low Countries and from abroad.

One such merchant was Lucas Rem, member of a patrician family in Augsburg. He visited Antwerp first in 1508, and spent much of his time conducting business there between 1511 and 1518. The happy coincidence of an entry in his diary and the Rem coat of arms on four landscape paintings that he must have acquired from the studio of Patinir permits a determination for the first time of the approximate date of several of the Master's works.[34]

---

[30] *Idem.*

[31] Van Mander makes this contradictory remark, which shows a confusion of Patinir and Met de Bles, in his account of the lives of the Brothers Frans and Gillis Mostaert (Mod. Dutch ed., p. 151).

[32] J. Helbig long ago denied the presence of this scatalogical detail in works by Patinir, noting that it did, however, occur in a painting, which he did not identify, by Lucas van Valckenborch (*op.cit.*, p. 467). A fine but much later landscape painter, Valckenborch gives prominence to such a figure in the foreground of *The*

Possessed of Gerasa (Brussels), signed and dated in 1597. It also occurs in a broad landscape painting of the *Martyrdom of St. Catherine* that was influenced by Patinir's treatment of the theme. This painting, which has been attributed to Pieter Bruegel as an early work, is in the National Gallery, Washington (Kress Coll., no. 1101).

[33] L. Guicciardini, *op.cit.*, p. 84. The Spaniards continued their substantial patronage of artists in Bruges (see G. Marlier, *Ambrosius Benson*, Damme, 1957, pp. 63-64).

[34] The diary was published and extensively

The diary reveals that Rem's extensive travels throughout Europe had three different motivations: he traveled for business to his warehouses in Lisbon, Lyon, Cologne, and Antwerp; for the sake of his soul's salvation to the pilgrimage sites of Rome, La Sainte-Baume in Southern France (locale of the hermitage of Mary Magdalene), and Monserrat in Spain; and for his poor health to the spa at Wildbad in South Germany. We read that his dealings in metals, wheat, cotton, spices, wine, and other commodities were so favorable in Portugal and France in 1516-17 that he was able to buy in Antwerp "paintings, gems, fabrics" and other luxury items, but that the years between 1502 and 1515 permitted no such extravagances.[35] Two of the landscapes that he presumably purchased from Patinir are today in the Philadelphia Museum. The first, in the John G. Johnson Collection, is a small, multi-scene composition featuring the *Assumption of the Virgin* (Fig. 20). The second is a small *Landscape with Preaching of John the Baptist*, formerly R. L. Taylor Collection (Fig. 11).[36] A third picture, *Landscape with St. Jerome*, is in the Ca d'Oro in Venice, and like the others is about twenty-two inches wide (Fig. 27).

Only the first of these, the *Assumption of the Virgin*, would seem on circumstantial evidence to have been specially commissioned by Rem. In the top framework of the picture, at the right, is the tiny grisaille figure of St. Luke, above his symbol the ox (Fig. 24). Luke was a patron saint of Lucas Rem, whose family name was the Biblical Hebrew word for wild ox (*reem*); and the black ox is twice pictured on his coat of arms. The other two paintings are copies of Patinir compositions which would either have been "on hand" in the studio or made to order for Rem.

The coat of arms and motto are superimposed on the landscape in the lower right-hand corner of each painting (Fig. 25). The black ox is rendered in profile facing left, on a gold shield, and again frontally above the helmet. On a ribbon surrounding the shield is Rem's pious motto in German, "ISTZ GVOT SO GEBS GO[T]" (If it is good, may God give it), a fitting one for a religious man of affairs, who ends his diary account of every difficult trip in his later years with "God be praised." Curiously, the motto on the *Landscape with Preaching of John the Baptist* is in Latin and expresses a different sentiment: "POST TENEBRAS SPERO LUC [EM?]." Since the arms

annotated by B. Greiff, *Tagebuch des Lucas Rem*, Augsburg, 1861. See also the entry on Rem in the *Allgemeine Deutsches Biographie*, XXVIII, Leipzig, 1889, p. 187. A portrait medallion of Rem by Friedrich Hagenauer is reproduced in Paul Wescher, *Grosskaufleute der Renaissance*, Basel, n.d., p. 135. An oil portrait of Rem, bearing his coat of arms and the date 1505, attributed to Leonhard Beck, is in Augsburg, Städtische Kunstsammlungen (illus. Exh. Cat. *Hans*

Holbein der Ältere und die Kunst der Spätgotik, Augsburg, 1965, no. 145, fig. 154).

[35] He did, however, spend "much money" in Portugal to acquire "new parrots, cats, and other rare and amusing things (*seltzam lustig Ding*)" (Greiff, *op.cit.*, p. 31).

[36] On the identification of the coat of arms see W. R. Valentiner, *Cat. of the John G. Johnson Coll.*, II, 1913, pp. 37-38, and III, 1914, p. 214; Friedländer, IX, 1931, no. 220, p. 156.

remain the same, the motto was presumably not the substitution of a later owner but was a second motto of Rem himself.[37]

Though the diary is silent about the further purchase by Rem of paintings in Antwerp after 1517, he made at least two further acquisitions, including his most important one. Apparently both were to commemorate his marriage on May 17, 1518, in Augsburg, to Anna Ochainin. The paintings would have been ordered when Rem was in Antwerp between September 1518 and January 1519, or between April and July 1520. He adds to his collection a fourth landscape by Patinir, which conforms in size with his others. He rounds out his collection of Patinir's most popular subjects with a *Rest on the Flight*, today in the collection of Mrs. George Kidston in Bristol, England (Fig. 19); and again it is an economy product from the Patinir workshop which utilizes pre-existing compositions by the Master. Rem's coat of arms and motto now appear in the lower left corner, with his wife's at the right (see Catalogue No. 20).

The second, more important purchase at this time was a triptych which Rem commissioned from Quentin Massys. Ordered no doubt as a donation, probably to a chapel in Augsburg, the altarpiece is today in the Pinakothek in Munich.[38] Prior to 1912, when a cleaning uncovered the arms of Rem and his wife, the work had sometimes been attributed, oddly enough, to Patinir even though the panels contain very little landscape.[39] M. J. Friedländer notes that the Altar depicts on the inner wings just those saints who spared Lucas Rem, his diary reports, from a terrible plague in 1505 in Portugal, Sebastian and Roch.[40] The exterior wings contain the grisaille figures of the name patrons of Rem and his bride, SS. Luke and Anne.

Thus, thanks to the diary of Lucas Rem, with its dated notation of the purchase

[37] As a matter of interesting coincidence, *Post tenebras lucem* was the motto of the morose King Philip II of Spain. See J. Dielitz, *Die Wahl und Denksprüche*, Frankfurt, 1884 (Kraus reprint, N.Y., 1963, p. 248).

[38] *Katalog der Alte Pinakothek, München*, 17th ed., 1930, pp. 91-92. The dimensions are 0.90 x 0.61 for the central panel, each wing 0.28 in width.

[39] The Rem arms were probably overpainted when the triptych was in the possession of the Elector Maximilian I of Bavaria. See Braune in *Münchner Jahrbuch*, IX, 1914-15, pp. 151-52, abb. 5-7.

[40] VII, 1921, pp. 48-49, taf. X. The central panel is unusual in composition, representing in juxtaposition the Trinity and the Madonna as the Apocalyptic Woman of the Sun. Though Rem does not refer in the diary to the commissioning of this altar, he begins the section that deals with his marriage with a reference to the Holy personages of the central panel; "Im namen der hayligen trivaltikaytt, Maria der edlen Junckfraw und gepererin und ales himlisch her" (Greiff, *op.cit.*, p. 43); and of the Lisbon plague he adds, "Gott durch forpitt [fürbitte] Maria seiner werden muetter, Sct. Sebastian und Sct. Rochus, aler gotz hayligen hat mich gar wunderperlich behiet" (*ibid.*, p. 9).

Baldass made an unsuccessful attempt to place the altar early among the works of Massys (dating it ca. 1508) in his excellent study "Gotik und Renaissance im Werke des Quinten Metsys," Vienna *Jahrbuch*, NF VII, 1933, pp. 160-63. This opinion has been recently rejected by K. G. Boon, *Quinten Massys*, Palet Series, Amsterdam, n.d., pp. 32-35. Massys' shop may have been responsible for much of the execution of the commission.

of paintings in Antwerp, and to Rem's rather uncommon desire to have the visible seal of ownership, his coat of arms, affixed to his property, we gain some insight not only into the chronology of the Patinir oeuvre but into his workshop procedure as well.

Our only other certain knowledge of the ownership of a picture by Patinir during the artist's lifetime was a small panel painting of Lot and his Daughters that was officially presented to Albrecht Dürer in Antwerp.[41] If this still exists today it might be the painting by Patinir now in Rotterdam, best titled *Landscape with Burning of Sodom* (Fig. 2).[42]

I have been able to determine the immediate destiny of none of the major works of Patinir. Unhappily, there is no coat of arms on the *Triptych with St. Jerome*, now in the Metropolitan Museum (Figs. 35, 38); but it seems likely that it too was commissioned by a South German merchant since the patron saint of Nuremberg, Sebald, appears in grisaille on an outer wing. In any event, it was later owned by the Hapsburgs and was given to the monastery of Kremsmunster, near Linz in Austria, in 1674 by Emperor Leopold I.[43]

The majority of Patinir's largest and finest paintings, no fewer than five, were acquired by King Philip II of Spain in the decades following the death of the artist; and all are still today in the Prado and Escorial,[44] along with the Most Catholic King's spectacular acquisitions of paintings by that other Netherlandish favorite of his, Hieronymus Bosch. The Escorial, begun in 1563, was ready in April 1574 to receive seventy-seven pictures, including Patinir's *Temptation of St. Anthony* (Fig. 44).[45] Upon completion of the great monastery-mausoleum in 1584, Patinir's *Landscape with St. Jerome* was sent to join the collection (Fig. 28).[46] The paintings would

[41] Note 3 above.

[42] Friedländer first made this suggestion (XIV, 1937, p. 119). See remarks under my entry of the Rotterdam painting in Catalogue 1, No. 3.

[43] The triptych remained in the monastery until 1936, when it was purchased by the Metropolitan Museum; H. B. Wehle, *op.cit.*, p. 80.

Another famous Hapsburg collector, Archduke Leopold Wilhelm of Austria, Governor of the Netherlands from 1646 to 1656, owned the two Patinir paintings today in the Kunsthistorisches Museum in Vienna: the signed *Baptism of Christ*, and the *Landscape with Martyrdom of St. Catherine*.

[44] In the Prado today: *Temptation of St. Anthony, Landscape with St. Jerome, Rest on the Flight*, and *Landscape with Charon's Boat*; and *St. Christopher*, in the Escorial.

[45] C. Justi, "Altflandrische Bilder in Spanien und Portugal, Joachim Patinier und Quentin Metsys," *Z.f.b.K.*, XXI, 1886, p. 93.

[46] This painting would have been especially

appropriate for the Escorial, where Philip II established a chapter of the Hieronymites. In 1605, Pater José de Sigüenza, historian of the Order, describes Patinir's picture as being in the lower cell of the prior:

"There are also pictures by a German or Fleming named Joachim. They are landscapes in oil although not very strongly drawn. One picture is the Miracle of the Five Thousand fed by the Lord in the desert with five loaves and two fish. He composed the picture so ingeniously that we can almost count them all. The other is our Doctor, St. Jerome, extracting a thorn from the foot of the lion. He put him in the desert and among some barren rocks. . . ." (*Historia de la Orden de San Jerónimo*, II, Madrid, 1909, p. 557; translated for me by Prof. Jonathan Brown). The picture of the Feeding of the Five Thousand to which Sigüenza refers, unidentifiable today, was probably incorrectly attributed to Patinir.

have been acquired by Philip himself, or his agents, by exchange, gift, or purchase from private ownership.[47] Some must have reached the Iberian peninsula before Philip began collecting. We have an attestation of the high regard in which the works of Patinir were held in Spain as early as ca. 1540, by Don Felipe de Guevara. He was a noted collector and painter, the son of Margaret of Austria's curator of tapestries, and friend of both Charles V and Philip II. In his *Comentarios de la Pintura* he named as the three greatest Flemish painters "Rugier (van der Weyden) y Joannes (van Eyck) y Joaquin Patinier."[48]

The productive career of Patinir, like that of Hugo van der Goes, was not a long one, apparently scarcely more than a dozen years. Our documentary knowledge of the man, and of his clientele, is nonetheless far richer than it is for a number of the important master painters of the Low Countries in the sixteenth century.

[47] It is possible that Philip acquired pictures even as a young man in his twenties, in 1549-51, when he visited the Low Countries for the first time (Justi, *loc.cit.*). He was again in his Northern realm from 1554 to 1559, though on this return trip the flagship, laden with paintings (one or more by Patinir?) and other treasure, sank in a storm (C. Petrie, *Philip II of Spain*, N.Y., 1963, pp. 57, 112).

[48] Published by Antonio Ponz, Madrid, 1788, p. 3; Friedländer, IX, p. 101.

CHAPTER TWO

THE MASTER AND HIS WORKSHOP

STYLE

UNLIKE that of several well-known painters of the early Netherlandish
school, the identity of Joachim Patinir did not have to be reestablished
in the nineteenth century.[1] To the contrary, a certain style of landscape
painting of the sixteenth century has always been associated with his name, though
frequently in confusion with that of his namesake, Herri de Patenier (met de Bles),
and of many anonymous followers. It is my purpose in this chapter to try to define
what I believe to be the Master's personal style of landscape painting and to estab-
lish his authentic oeuvre. This reappraisal is needed, especially in view of the fact
that scholarly attributions of pictures to him have been much too freely made—more
perhaps than for most old masters.[2]

Although the influence of Bosch on Patinir has long been recognized, it has
been rather underestimated in the literature, while at the same time that of Gerard
David has perhaps been unduly stressed.[3] That David and Patinir were enrolled
together as freemasters in the Antwerp guild in 1515 in itself probably means little;
and there is no reason to conjecture that Patinir was trained in Bruges by David.[4]
David's influence was comparatively superficial, restricted almost entirely to a number of motifs which Patinir adopts for his own interpretations of two themes, the
Flight into Egypt and the Baptism of Christ.

[1] Bibliographies of the earliest literature on the
artist are given in Wurzbach, *Niederländisches
Künstler-Lexikon*, II, 1910, p. 311 and III, 1911,
p. 131; Thieme-Becker, XXVI, 1932, p. 293; and
H.-W. von Löhneysen, *Künstler und Kritiker*,
Eisenach, 1956, pp. 388-92.

[2] For example by L. van Puyvelde, *La peinture flamande au siècle de Bosch et Breughel*,
Paris (Elsevier/Meddens), 1962, p. 223. There
have been two very sound studies, limited only
in scope, of the style of Patinir: L. Baldass, "Die
niederländische Landschaftsmalerei von Patinir
bis Bruegel," Vienna *Jahrbuch*, XXXIV, 1918, pp.
113-22 (hereafter cited as "L. Baldass, 1918"),
and M. J. Friedländer in *From van Eyck to
Bruegel*, N.Y. (Phaidon Press), (1916, 1st German edition), 1956, pp. 76ff. (hereinafter cited
simply by year of publication), and in *Die Altniederländische Malerei*, IX, 1931, pp. 101-24
(hereafter cited simply by volume number).

Other studies include M. Conway, *The Van
Eycks and their Followers*, New York, 1921,
pp. 348ff.; C. van de Wetering, *Die Entwicklung der niederländische Landschaftsmalerei
vom Anfang des 16. Jahrhunderts bis zur Jahrhundertmitte*, Berlin, 1938, pp. 24-30; André
Lhote, *Treatise on Landscape Painting* (tr. W. J.
Strachan), London, 1950, passim; Yvonne
Thiéry, *Le paysage flamand au xvii siècle*, Paris,
1953, introductory chapter on the 16th century
background; and G. J. Hoogewerff, *Het Landschap van Bosch tot Rubens*, Antwerp, 1954, pp.
17-27. The landscape style of Bosch has been
studied by G. van Camp, "Considérations sur le
Paysage chez Jérôme Bosch," *Miscellanea Leo
van Puyvelde*, Brussels, 1949, pp. 65-73.

[3] Notably by Baldass, 1918. Friedländer, on
the other hand, does not minimize the influence
of Bosch (IX, pp. 109-11).

[4] Conway, *loc.cit.*

From Bosch, on the other hand, Patinir derived his basic orientation to land-scape, a preference in subject matter for penitent saints in the wilderness, numerous formulae and iconographical details, and even to a certain degree his technique of painting. So strong was the influence of the Master of s'Hertogenbosch that one would like to believe that Patinir's early training took place not at Bruges but instead in this outpost in North Brabant. While this is possible, since Bosch did not die until 1516, it is not probable, for though he had many imitators Bosch is not known to have trained pupils. It is reasonable to assume only that Patinir was able to derive his style from a persevering study of the paintings of Bosch. The influence may be felt already in such early works by Patinir as the *Flight into Egypt* (Fig. 4), *Burning of Sodom* (Fig. 2), and the *Martyrdom of St. Catherine* (Figs. 6-7), all probably painted before Patinir's enrollment in the Antwerp guild. Since Antwerp is the most likely place, outside s'Hertogenbosch itself, for Patinir to have seen a number of paintings by Bosch, it is tempting to believe that he might have been trained in Antwerp before his name appears in 1515 as freemaster in the records of that city's guild of painters.[5] In any case the influence of paintings by Bosch continues through-out the middle period of Patinir's career in Antwerp and reaches a climax in the late landscapes depicting *Christopher* (Fig. 49), the *Temptation of St. Anthony* (Fig. 44), and *Charon's Boat* (Fig. 54), masterworks which succeed in evoking the very mood of Bosch.

The most striking compositional device that Patinir derives from Bosch is the unusually high eye level, frequently involving a very elevated horizon line, from which his world landscape is viewed. This is new only in the matter of degree, for an elevated vantage point had been a principle that controlled the landscape in the background of Flemish compositions since the early years of the fifteenth century. It helped to create the desired effect of continuity of space, extending to a far distance from an immediate foreground where the *dramatis personnae* perform. But even with the high horizon the problem of representing the middle distance remains a major one throughout the fifteenth century and into the next. Gerard David often avoids a middle ground by lowering the eye-level, sometimes dramatically, in order

---

[5] Dr. Henri Pauwels, who kindly checked for me the registry of those persons who acquired citizenship rights in Antwerp between Oct. 1, 1503, and Sept. 30, 1517, did not encounter the name of Joachim Patinir (Brussels, Rijksarchief, Rekenkamer, document entitled *Binnenpoorters*). I agree with the following evaluation of this fact, with respect to the possibility of Patinir's presence in Antwerp before his enrollment in the painters' guild in 1515: "Il faut noter que je n'ai pas non plus trouvé mention du nom de Gérard David. Faut-il en conclure que le séjour de G. David a été de très courte durée, ou tout simplement que, pour une raison qui nous échappe, tous ceux qui s'installaient dans cette ville n'étaient pas obligés ou n'achetaient pas le droit de bourgeoisie? Le silence de ces documents au sujet de Patinir ne me semble en tout cas pas exclure *a priori* la présence de ce peintre à Anvers avant 1515." I am grateful to Prof. Sadja Herzog for calling my attention to the existence of this document.

to give a relationship of figures to space which is more realistic optically. When he elects to extend the middle distance on an upward sloping ground, as in the *Baptism Triptych* (Bruges), which impressed Patinir, he can give little more than a glimpse of a far distance.[6] At the same time, Patinir deliberately chooses the bird's-eye view in order to create a vast stage of operations, following the lead of Bosch in his panoramic triptychs. The Master varies his point of vantage from a very high elevation (*Martyrdom of St. Catherine*, Fig. 6; *Ecstasy of Mary Magdalene*, Fig. 32), to one very nearly at his own ground level (*Baptism of Christ*, Fig. 8; *Christopher*, Fig. 49). Moreover, he frequently finds it desirable to continue the old Flemish system of an elevated foreground plateau, even in a number of the late works (Metropolitan Museum *Triptych*, Fig. 35; *Temptation of St. Anthony*, Fig. 44).[7]

In a somewhat cartographic fashion two different perspective principles operate together in a Patinir landscape. Horizontal elements (fields, bodies of water, roads, and sometimes forests) are seen from above, while vertical elements (farmhouses, buildings, distant cities, rocks, and single trees) are seen more or less at eye level. These two perspectives are operative regardless of the distance of the object from the eye of the spectator. Patinir exploits this system in an effort to bring order and clarity to the multitudinous detail in his landscape. One reads the composition as an additive series of diminishing views or vignettes, one on top of another as they recede into space. This had been practiced earlier in North Italian painting, sometimes in a very dramatic fashion, though frequently without an interest in spatial recession. Vital to the unity of Patinir's composition is the careful ordering of all of the vertical components parallel to the picture plane, as M. J. Friedländer has pointed out.[8] This may best be observed in his largest pictures, but it operates as well in the smaller ones, such as the *Martyrdom of St. Catherine* (Fig. 6). Here the vista is boldly organized in a series of diagonals from left to right; but because most of the pictorial elements are parallel to the picture plane one reads the composition vertically as well as diagonally into depth. It is as though the river valley had suffered a geological fault, shifting the port city forty-five degrees, while leaving it miraculously intact.

When they are large, the figure or figures which comprise the subject of Patinir's paintings are placed as a rule near the central foreground. When small, they may be displaced to one side, giving way to the landscape (*Burning of Sodom*, Fig. 2). In such a case the staffage is usually placed, for emphasis, before a rock mass, and this creates a composition that is asymmetrical and dynamically imbalanced. With the weight on one side, the other invariably opens to a distant space that is closed

[6] See Baldass, "Gerard David als Landschafts-maler," Vienna *Jahrbuch*, NF x, 1936, pp. 89ff.

[7] For an interesting interpretation of the "foreground plateau" in early Flemish painting see M. Meiss, "Highlands in the Lowlands," *G.d.B.-A.*, LVII, 1961, pp. 273-314.

[8] IX, p. 107.

not by pictorial elements within the composition but only by the frame itself (Prado *Jerome*, Fig. 28). If the composition is controlled by a central mass, there may be middle distant vistas of special landscape interest on both sides (Prado *Rest on the Flight*, Fig. 39); or a combination of middle and far distant views (Louvre *Jerome*, Fig. 26); or far distant views on both sides (Berlin *Rest on the Flight*, Fig. 40). These modes of composition point the way to the development of Flemish landscape in the later sixteenth century far more than does the final compositional scheme employed by Patinir: an unimpeded sweep back into space across the picture plane (*Christopher*, Fig. 49; *Temptation of Anthony*, Fig. 44; *Charon's Boat*, Fig. 54). These are the Master's least complicated yet most sophisticated and accomplished landscapes, and they adumbrate the development of landscape painting in the Lowlands of the seventeenth century.

In every Western landscape painting before the nineteenth century, the illusion of distance was created in principle by the diminution of scale and a progressive loss of clarity; but Patinir is inclined to mock this law of aerial perspective until the eye of the spectator is close to the horizon line (Metropolitan Museum *Triptych*, Fig. 35). In other words, he permits us to scan the landscape as though through a telescope. Sometimes the scale changes irrationally and abruptly, as for example in the monastic establishment of Jerome on the rocky promontory in the Prado version (Fig. 28). Or he may employ the stage-like device of the coulisse, used with such great effect by Quentin Massys. In this scheme distant space is brought into dramatic juxtaposition with the foreground, as in the pocket of space to the right of Jerome in the Metropolitan Museum *Triptych* (Fig. 35). In the immediate foreground he frequently places plants, animals, rocks, a flow of spring water, or still-life objects, as a means of relating the viewer to the picture space. To increase the illusion, they are greatly detailed and painted in very sharp focus. Another means of giving scale, and a yardstick for the measure of depth, is the isolated tree that is sometimes placed in the foreground. It is usually either dead, probably for symbolic reasons, or else given sparse foliage so as not to obscure the distant view. The isolated tree was perhaps introduced into Flemish painting by Bosch in the *John on Patmos* (Berlin),[9] though Patinir brings to it a better though still imperfect scale relationship to the foreground figure, and thereby to the landscape, by sometimes allowing its upper branches to be cut from view by the picture frame (*Baptism of Christ*, Fig. 8).

The lighting of the landscape is artificial and rather arbitrary in the nearer distances, relying a great deal on the contrast of color values for its effect; and the transition to a bright far distance is sometimes abrupt. While the lighting tends to be flat, for the sake of over-all clarity, tree foliage and rocks are usually accented in

[9] This observation was made by Fierens-Gevaert (cited by J. Lassaigne and R. Delevoy, *La peinture flamande de Jérôme Bosch à Rubens*, Geneva, 1958, p. 28).

light and shadow. The leafage of the unusually compact, trimly rounded, distant trees is modeled by stippling in dots or flecks of light against dark, a technique used by Bosch, Memling, and others before him. Masses of painstakingly dotted trees produce a striking effect in a Patinir composition, and it is interesting to note that Van Mander elected to specify the landscape style of the Master only by the fact that his trees were *getippelt*. Cast shadows are infrequent, and his human beings and animals either cast no shadows at all or very weak ones, once again perhaps a reflection of the technique of Bosch.

Overlapping folds of earth, like stage flats, are continued from the earlier tradition, though with more of an emphasis placed on modeling. Light and dark values are opposed in two ways. Either the base of the ground swell is bright and darkens at the summit (Karlsruhe *Jerome*, Fig. 1), or vice versa. In either case a contour line is created when dark and light meet, clarifying the earth mass. Both may be found in combination behind the Madonna in the Prado *Rest on the Flight* (Fig. 39).

Dark colors, especially deep blue and green, play an important role in the Patinir landscape. He goes beyond David and Bosch in handling the so-called formula of the "three distances," which is to remain more or less the rule in Flemish landscape painting throughout the sixteenth century. The scheme called for a predominantly reddish brown foreground, a green middle distance, and a blue far distance. These three basic hues are greatly varied, supplemented, and intermixed in order to effect a natural transition between the zones and to enrich a given area. For instance, in the foreground plants of the *Temptation of Anthony* (Fig. 44) there is a marvelous color range from black-green through subtle variations of green and brown to a faded gold. The foreground and middle distance frequently contain blue-gray or purplish rocks, sometimes tinged with ochre; and houses are brightened in variegated pastel hues that are mostly of a red or yellow cast. The far distant blue permits little color play, though Patinir varies its intensity and may shade it to green or gray. Bright red may occur in its traditional role as the local color of the costume of a foreground figure, and touches of it may also spark the sky, or a distant earthly or infernal fire. The sky is usually shaded from a bright, creamy tone on the horizon through white and bluish white to a deep azure blue at the frame. With few exceptions the sky is filled with white cumulus clouds, evoking the mood of a clear, late summer afternoon, the atmosphere cleared of dust by a recent rain. Sometimes the clouds may assume the stormy colors of deep blue, black, and red, when Patinir wishes to express the anger of God (*Burning of Sodom*, Fig. 2), or the dark night of the soul of a wilderness saint (*Temptation of Anthony*, Fig. 44); Metropolitan Museum, *Triptych with St. Jerome*, Fig. 35).

From the trickle of a foreground stream to rivers that empty in the foreground

or meander in the distance, from ponds and lakes to great bays, water is an important element of the Master's world landscape. According to its character, the surface of the water may be smooth or gently rippled, but never angry, even though the stories of Christopher and of Charon's boat would have permitted such a treatment. Sometimes, without consistency, the water reflects the elements of earth, and often it is a luminous and limpid mirror of the sky, as in that boldly contrived tour-de-force, *Charon's Boat* (Fig. 54).

Natural rock formations are very important in Patinir's scheme. They are especially dramatic in the earlier paintings and are used with great effect even when they are not central to the theme (*Martyrdom of St. Catherine*, Fig. 6; *Baptism of Christ*, Fig. 8). While Bosch invents rock fantasies and David represents neatly quarried rocky embankments, Patinir commemorates the rocky country of his birth. He was evidently deeply affected by the noted landmarks along the Meuse River around Namur and Dinant: the Marche-les-Dames, a bright gray wall which rises precipitously from the river; the bluish limestone Rochers de Frènes; and the dramatic chimney-like Bayard Rock at Dinant.[10] What appear to be melodramatic rock fantasies in Patinir's paintings are really constructions based upon his personal observation of nature. He defies optical reality, however, in giving as much detail to rocky masses that are far distant as to those that are nearby. Patinir willfully disrupts scale in order to make his landscape more immediate and more exciting.

Even though individual objects, especially when seen at close range, are rendered with that love of descriptive realism that had been the birthright of Netherlandish masters since the early fifteenth century, Patinir's landscape style cannot be called "realistic." Working "a bit like an architect and a bit like a cartographer"[11] in constructing his vast vistas of space, he was either disinterested in or unaware of scientific rules of perspective, which in any event would have availed him little in his conquest of landscape. It is in fact the very two-dimensional quality of a painting by Patinir, the Prado *Landscape with St. Jerome* (Fig. 28), that excites the modern French painter André Lhote, who has reacted to it with the following words:

> "Nothing evanescent or inaccessible; the clouds on the horizon are as
> clear as the earth of the foreground. The great mass of dark rocks at the
> center, cut out against a broad, clear vista, is violently projected on to the
> same plane as the ground where the saint's hut is perched, and the last clear
> rock which terminates the composition on the left, similarly pushed back by

[10] That Patinir's landscape derived from the "grand, broken scenery" of the valley of the Meuse was noted as long ago as 1845 by A. van Lokeren (cited by J. A. Crowe in a revision of Waagen's ed. of Kugler, *The German, Flemish and Dutch Schools*, London, 1911, p. 123).

[11] Friedländer, IX, p. 124.

the vast triangular cloud drawn behind it like a piece of somber drapery, is miraculously placed on the same level as the two preceding planes, that is, on the plane of the picture itself. . . . It is because of their rediscovery of this science of compensations of volumes that Cézanne, Renoir, and Seurat were so great."[12]

CHRONOLOGY AND ICONOGRAPHY

I believe that there are fewer than twenty paintings, in public and private collections in Europe and the United States, that should be ascribed to Patinir himself. Five of these bear what would appear to be genuine signatures. In addition I have catalogued about twenty-five other pictures that bear a close relationship to the works of the Master. Some of these were surely produced in his workshop, and they fall into three categories: 1) replicas of about the same size; 2) copies involving a change in size and in detail; and 3) new compositions which carefully copy and/or combine motifs invented by Patinir. These putative workshop paintings will be discussed later in this chapter.

The relatively small number of extant "originals" is not improbable for a number of reasons. The principal one is that Patinir seems to have suffered a premature death, and hence he may have had a productive span of scarcely more than a dozen years. Twenty paintings, nearly half of which are of relatively large size, is a not improbable oeuvre when one considers the greatly detailed nature of his work and the laborious technique of multiple glazes which was his heritage, and which he elected to continue. Furthermore, though Patinir conducted a workshop in Antwerp there is little reason to think that it was an especially large one. It would also be unreasonable to believe that many paintings by this Master have not survived the ages. As most were not altarpieces, they would have been inoffensive, as well as unavailable, to the iconoclasts who ravaged the Low Countries in the dark year of 1566. Further, by the 1560's most of Patinir's best paintings would already have been sent to Spain and to Germany, as has been mentioned.

Although no painting bears a date, an arrangement of the works in an approximate chronological order is possible in spite of the brief span of time in which they were painted. Both the formative style and the most mature style have been recognized by almost every critic, for they are easily defined.[13] With few exceptions my arrangement agrees basically with that made by Ludwig Baldass fifty years ago, and it has been necessary to interpolate only a few paintings that were not known to him, and to exclude one or two others.[14]

[12] *Op.cit.,* pp. 15-16. Tr. Strachan.

[13] L. Baldass, 1918, pp. 113-22; M. J. Friedländer, IX, pp. 101-24. Another attempt to arrange the works in chronological order is that of G. J. Hoogewerff, in *Het Landscap van Bosch tot Rubens,* Antwerp, 1954, pp. 17-27. In my opinion it makes little sense.

[14] Baldass, *loc.cit.,* puts the Lugano *Rest on*

Circumstantial evidence makes it possible to give approximate dates to four paintings of the middle and late periods. As discussed in the first chapter, the German merchant Lucas Rem probably commissioned from Patinir the *Assumption of the Virgin* (Fig. 20) in 1516-17. Perhaps at the same time he acquired a small copy, today in the Ca d'Oro, of the Louvre *Landscape with Jerome* (Fig. 27) and also a replica, now in Philadelphia, of the Brussels *Preaching of John the Baptist* (Fig. 11). Again in Antwerp in 1520, after his marriage, Rem may have ordered the *Rest on the Flight* (Fig. 19) today in the Kidston Collection (Bristol), a composition combining the landscapes of the Kaufmann-Kaus Triptych and Prado *Rest on the Flight*. In each case the copy for Rem would provide a *terminus ante quem* for its prototype, and thus we gain a putative date of 1520 for the Prado *Rest* (Fig. 39). Quite probably the Escorial *St. Christopher* (Fig. 49) should be placed in, or shortly after, 1521 because of its dependence upon an engraving and figure drawings made by Dürer for Patinir in that year.[15] Finally, I would propose a date of around 1522 for Patinir's collaboration with Quentin Massys on the *Temptation of St. Anthony* (Fig. 44), since the date 1522 appears on a large woodcut by Jan de Cock which evidently was influenced by the painting.[16] None of these dates would be inconsistent with my proposed chronology.

The Early Period consists, I believe, of four relatively small pictures, painted before the enrollment of Patinir as freemaster in the Antwerp guild in 1515. The next six years may be said to comprise a Middle Period in which a fully mature landscape style gives the appearance of a more or less unified whole through the ordering of single motifs. The bulk of his work, including many of the known copies and adaptations, falls within this productive span from 1515 to 1519. A Late Period, commencing in 1520 and terminated by the artist's death in 1524, would contain the four masterpieces in which the world landscape is presented as a fully unified view and on a grand scale.

---

the Flight much earlier in Patinir's career than I do. Another point of difference between us is his attribution to Patinir of an *Ecstasy of Mary Magdalene* (illus. in Friedländer, IX, taf. CII, as Patinir), a painting formerly in the Crespi Coll. in Milan.

Friedländer has made the only attempt to catalogue the entire oeuvre as he knew it (Vol. IX, pp. 156-59; nos. 218-57; addenda in Vol. XIV, 1937, pp. 118-19). Of the 39 pictures, plus seven copies and replicas, which comprise his 1931 list in Vol. IX, I have categorically rejected four as being connected with neither Patinir

nor his workshop: no. 224 (now in the Portland, Oregon, Art Museum), nos. 225, 225a (the same picture, now in the Brussels Museum), nos. 227, 227a, and 252). I have reattributed three to the Master of the Half-Lengths: nos. 222-23 (now joined), no. 244 (now in Kansas City, Nelson Gallery), no. 256. No. 257 (Coll. Sir Robert Thomas) I believe to be in the style of Isenbrandt. I have been unable to trace nine pictures: nos. 220b, 229, 230, 233, 238, 242, 247, 249, and 255.

[15] See Chapter III, p. 50, n. 3.

[16] The relationship is discussed below, p. 40.

Were it not signed, the little Karlsruhe *Jerome* (Fig. 1) would probably be regarded as the feeble work of an imitator of the style of Patinir; and it would, therefore, have found no place in this monograph. But the inscription (in the lower left corner) appears to be genuine, making this a unique instance in which the first known work of an early Netherlandish painter bears a signature. However weakly executed, the composition contains the basic elements of Patinir's landscape structure, and much of his landscape iconography; and thus we are given the unusual opportunity to observe the genesis of what was soon to develop into a fine style. Not much larger than a postcard, the composition marks the beginning of motifs that will be frequently repeated: the pairs of travelers wandering about the countryside, Jerome's monastery church, Flemish farmhouses, a crumbling stone viaduct arch, and a steep outcropping of rocks for landscape accent. In the center of the composition, the kneeling, bearded penitent beats his bared chest with a stone as he holds an opened book and prays before a crucifix propped against a stump. This general iconographic type of Jerome ultimately descended from Italian representations, and it very likely reached Patinir through Dürer's famous engraving of 1496-97 (B 61). There are also a number of analogies with Bosch's *Altarpiece of the Hermit Saints* (Doges' Palace, Venice).[17] The importance of Patinir's composition, however, resides in the fact that presumably for the first time in Netherlandish panel painting an artist dared to create a "Landscape with Saint Jerome" instead of the conventional "Saint Jerome in a landscape."

The other three pictures of the early period are stylistically homogeneous: the Antwerp *Flight into Egypt* (Fig. 4), Rotterdam *Burning of Sodom* (Fig. 2), and Vienna *Martyrdom of St. Catherine* (Figs. 6-7). As a compositional development from the Karlsruhe painting, all three exploit naked rock formations which rise at an angle from an elevated foreground almost to the top of the picture plane, on one side of the composition. They frame a landscape view in which the water of a bay meets the sky at a high and distant horizon.

A little larger than the Karlsruhe *Jerome*, and also signed, the Antwerp *Flight into Egypt* (Fig. 4) represents a marked technical advance in its better modeling, more unified lighting, and especially in the proliferation of landscape detail that will remain a hallmark of Patinir's style. Under the inspiration of the technique of Bosch, he enlivens the greenish and reddish brown earth of the foreground hill with dots of sparkling light, while the far distance is gradually absorbed by the bright light of the sky. The sketchy draughtsmanship of the little figures of the Holy Family, whose peasant-like appearance lends a startlingly new note of reality to

---

[17] The Bosch triptych is reproduced, for example, in L. Baldass, *H. Bosch*, New York, 1960, pl. 76.

EARLY PERIOD, TO 1514

PROVENIENCE	SUBJECT	CAT. NO.	FIG.
Karlsruhe, Kunsthalle	*Landscape with St. Jerome*	I	I
Antwerp, Museum	*Landscape with Flight into Egypt*	2	4, 5
Rotterdam, Boymans-Van Beuningen Museum	*Landscape with Burning of Sodom*	3	2
Vienna, Kunsthistorisches Museum	*Landscape with Martyrdom of St. Catherine*	4	6, 7

MIDDLE PERIOD, 1515-1519

PROVENIENCE	SUBJECT	CAT. NO.	FIG.
Vienna, Kunsthistorisches Museum	*Baptism of Christ*	5	8, 9
Brussels, Museum	*Landscape with Preaching of John the Baptist*	6	10
Lugano, Thyssen Coll.	*Landscape with Rest on the Flight*	7	12
Frankfurt, Kaus Coll. (formerly Kaufmann Coll.)	*Triptych with Rest on the Flight*	8	16, 17, 18
Philadelphia, Johnson Coll.	*Assumption of the Virgin*	9	20, 22, 23, 24, 25
Paris, Louvre	*Landscape with St. Jerome*	10	26
Madrid, Prado	*Landscape with St. Jerome*	11	28, 29
London, National Gallery	*Landscape with St. Jerome*	12	30
Zurich, Kunsthaus	*Landscape with Ecstasy of Mary Magdalene* (copy?)	13	32
New York, Metropolitan Museum	*Triptych with St. Jerome*	14	35, 37, 38
Berlin-Dahlem, Museum	*Rest on the Flight*	15	40

LATE PERIOD, 1520-1524

PROVENIENCE	SUBJECT	CAT. NO.	FIG.
Madrid, Prado	*Rest on the Flight*	16	39 41, 42, 43
Madrid, Prado	*Temptation of St. Anthony*	17	44, 45, 46, 47
Escorial	*St. Christopher*	18	49, 50, 51, 52
Madrid, Prado	*Landscape with Charon's Boat*	19	54, 55, 56

an old theme, is at least partly intentional, since they are no longer the real *raison d'être* of the picture.[18] Story-telling details invite the viewer to roam the countryside. At the extreme left a pagan idol falls from its pedestal to bear witness to the power of the Child,[19] while the Biblical Massacre of the Innocents is combined with the legendary story of the miraculous field of wheat before the farmhouses at the right.[20] Timidly realized in this early composition, these episodes will be given great emphasis in later paintings. Beneath the trees behind the Holy Family is a pair of rabbits, peaceful creatures that Patinir will use almost as a signature in the future. One rabbit turns its back to us as in Dürer's 1504 engraving of Adam and Eve (B 1), a print that may also have inspired the use of a mountain goat, silhouetted against the sky on a distant rock. A pair of swans on the pond at the right are others of an animal kingdom that Patinir will augment in the future.

The *Burning of Sodom* (Fig. 2), with its twin-city Gomorrah afire in the far distance, is like a page from Bosch from which the grotesque images have been erased. The entire sky is red, and the Dead Sea is a lake of blood, played against a dark green foreground and bright gray-and-ochre rocks. In the exact center of the composition is the stony image of Lot's wife (appropriately named "Pierra" in the French mystery plays of Patinir's day), while at the extreme right are the tiny figures of Lot and his two daughters being hastened to safety by white-winged angels. That this painting belongs to the early period is attested by the comparative lack of skill in integrating the various elements of the composition within the landscape; for example, the chateau afire near the left foreground seems to exist in a perspectival space of its own. The same may also be said of the tent with Lot and his daughters, tucked away for safety near the right edge of the composition. With a characteristically Netherlandish disregard for those principles that govern classical compositional design, Patinir will always tend to bring story-telling details to the very borders, and far back into the depth, of a landscape. The jagged, dramatically lighted rocks with a

[18] Patinir may have been familiar with Schongauer's engraving *Peasant Family Going to Market* (L 90), the figure group being similar in design.

[19] The incident of the falling idol is from Pseudo-Matthew, Ch. XXIII.

[20] The legend of the wheatfield has not been traced to its original source. The field of ripened grain sprang up overnight to impede the progress of the soldiers of Herod as they sought the Holy Family; and the episode appears in art as early as the 11th century. Apart from manuscript miniatures of the Flemish school, it occurs in a painting perhaps known to Patinir,

Memling's *Seven Joys of Mary* (Munich), dating ca. 1480. A detail of this is reproduced, and further literature on the legend given, by H. Wentzel, "Die Kornfeldlegende," *Festschrift Kurt Bauch*, Deutscher Kunstverlag, n.d. (1957), p. 182, fig. 5.

One detail will be repeated by Patinir in all of his later versions of the theme, that of the soldier with drawn sword in pursuit of a mother clutching her child. In one of these (the Kaufmann-Kaus Triptych) the figure of a woman with her arms raised in horror may also have derived from Memling's painting.

tunnel through them will reappear on a grand scale as the setting for compositions with St. Jerome.

For the *Martyrdom of St. Catherine* (Figs. 6-7) the artist conceives an extended bird's-eye view of a busy port city, as it might be recorded by a camera with a wide-angle lens. It is viewed from a hilltop, the foreground rocks cut by the picture frame in a manner without precedence in Flemish painting. The swarm of colorfully dressed and armed malefactors who flee in panic from the fiery, broken torture wheels have been inspired by the exotic symbols of evil that Bosch had created. A ploughman in the valley flees in fright at the approach of the armed horde, while on the riverbank within the walls of the city a crowd has gathered to witness the auto-da-fé of the fifty philosophers who had been converted to Christianity by the Alexandrian Princess Catherine, and who were then burned because they could not answer her arguments against worship of idols. The scene in the mountains represents not the actual martyrdom of Catherine but rather its prelude. Thus the angel that descends in a burst of light, brandishing two swords, announces both the intervention of God and the impending death of the Saint by decapitation. Patinir makes of Alexandria, as he had of Sodom, an almost completely Flemish city, not for symbolic reasons but in the interest of identification on the part of the viewers of the picture. Ships are being built and repaired on the opposite bank of the river, carrack merchantmen have unloaded barrels at the wharves, and three-masted caravels are to be seen in the outer harbor. Within the city is the large, circular "temple of Solomon" that had symbolized Jerusalem in Netherlandish painting since the time of the Van Eycks. Nearby, and towering above it, is a splendid Gothic church.

After these essays in small-size pictures on wooden panels, compositions in which for the first time in Flemish painting landscape is permitted to predominate over staffage, Patinir undertakes big landscape paintings. The stimulus may have been given in 1515 by his acceptance as freemaster in the Antwerp Guild of Painters.

MIDDLE PERIOD

It has been debated whether Patinir himself painted the figures which are displayed in solemn and traditional fashion in the foregrounds of the *Baptism of Christ* in Vienna (Fig. 8), and in the Kaus (formerly Kaufmann) Triptych now in Frankfurt (Figs. 16-18). The difficult problem of Patinir as figure painter is the subject of the next chapter. Friedländer was convinced long ago that the Master himself did paint the figures in both of these compositions, a conviction strengthened by the fact that the *Baptism* is signed, on a rock in the foreground, as the "opus" of Patinir (and no one else).[21] Patinir was surely capable of painting figures, and there

---

[21] IX, p. 105.

is no reason to doubt that he painted the picturesque group to which the Baptist preaches in the middle distance (Fig. 9, detail). These figures are very close in style to the little figures in the *Martyrdom of St. Catherine*, which are so much a part of the landscape that it would be hard to believe that Patinir did not paint them himself. The monumental figures of Christ and St. John are firmly affixed to the picture plane, so to speak, and bear a somewhat tenuous relationship to the landscape that spreads out behind them. The two are repeated in the middle distance, as John points out to the unknowing crowd the nearby figure that is their Saviour. The time-honored pictorial violation of the unity of time, whereby the story-telling content of the composition could be enriched, perfectly suited Patinir's interest in bringing distant landscape to life, and life to distant landscape. Both figure groups were directly inspired by the famous Triptych of the Baptism that Gerard David painted in 1502-3 in Bruges; and from the same source Patinir takes the yellow water-iris behind Christ, a flower that he will almost always include in future compositions. Beyond David, Patinir makes a new and bold attempt—however imperfectly real-ized—to integrate figures and landscape by the tree at the left, its top cut from view by the picture frame. It is nearly dead, and there are a thistle plant and salamanders at its base. The Jordan empties into the foreground, and our eye slowly charts its flow, against the current, into the depth of the landscape. It swings to the right, past a family of deer, a fisherman, and the ruins of a castle on a rock. The river dis-appears behind a spectacular rocky mass which rises to the figure of God, white-bearded and holding a giant crystal orb. He has dispatched the Dove of the Holy Ghost; and thus the Trinity precisely commands the central axis of the composition. The river continues its meandering course at the left, silhouetting against its mirror-smooth surface the tiny figure of Christ to whom the Baptist points. Farther on are two merchants with pack-camels, a colorful detail borrowed from the story of St. Jerome in the wilderness. The rolling hills and fields of the far distance are speckled with dwellings and tiny figures, inviting the viewer to inspect the picture at very close range, as in the painting of Jan van Eyck.

Similar in style, and a key work in the early mature style of Patinir, is the *Triptych with Rest on the Flight*, which was in the Kaufmann Collection in Berlin before it was damaged by fire in 1904 (Figs. 16-18). Restored, it is today in the Collection of Willy Kaus in Frankfurt.[22] The altarpiece had been exhibited in the great Bruges exhibition of Flemish art in 1902, and Hulin de Loo called it "an important and characteristic work of the Master," insisting that the landscape derived from Bosch, not David, and that Patinir himself painted the figures of the Madonna and Child, Joseph (who fills a canteen from the miraculous spring), and the figures of John the Baptist and St. Pope Cornelius on either wing.[23] Baldass and Friedländer accepted

---

[22] On its history see Catalogue I, No. 8.   [23] *Catalogue critique*, p. 54.

the altarpiece without reservations as a work by Patinir.[24] While I am more hesitant and feel that it may be a collaborative undertaking of Patinir and an unidentified master, it is evident that Patinir was responsible for the glorious landscape of the central panel. It was highly esteemed, and his workshop produced two smaller, rectangular adaptations of it, one made for Lucas Rem (and now in the Collection of Mrs. George Kidston in Bristol [Fig. 19]), and the other a close copy of the background alone, in a painting now in the Minneapolis Museum (Fig. 21). The St. John who stands on the left wing is a twin of the one who kneels in the foreground of the Vienna *Baptism* (Fig. 8). Behind him are the episodes of the Preaching in the Wilderness and the Baptism. Patinir had made these the subject of an independent landscape picture, today in the Brussels Museum (Fig. 10); and once again Lucas Rem wished a copy, now in the Philadelphia Museum (Fig. 11).

The narrow landscape of the Baptist wing has two features not typical of Patinir. The framing of either edge of the composition with a leafy tree is found again in the Patinir "milieu" only in the problematic *Landscape with Shepherds* (Fig. 69), which I believe was painted by a follower; further, nowhere else in his certain works are distant rocks piled up with openings to the sky. On the other hand the rock bridge open to the sky was a motif current in the Antwerp school at this time, and it may be found very frequently in paintings attributed to Quentin Massys and Joos van Cleve.[25]

In the central panel of the Kaufmann-Kaus Triptych the episodes of the Massacre of the Innocents and the Miraculous Wheatfield have been developed far beyond a timid introduction in the Antwerp composition to become an almost independent genre scene of country life. Its details, some of which remind us of Bosch, will be repeated in various combinations by Patinir himself, and by his workshop: the ploughman with oxen, a farmer leading a horse-drawn harrow, shepherds with their flock on a distant hill (here one performs a handstand as two sheep stray), a woman bearing a water jar on her head, and a sow with litter. Most prominent is the carefully rendered ploughman with the team of two oxen, one white and the other brown. This motif was taken directly from the calendar picture for March in the Chantilly *Book of Hours*, commissioned by the Duke of Berry in the early fifteenth century.[26] This sumptuous manuscript had passed through inheritance to Margaret of Austria

[24] Baldass, 1918, p. 117; Friedländer, IX, pp. 115-16.

[25] C. de Tolnay has pointed out that the rock-arch motif began in antiquity and reappears in the 15th century Ferrarese School ("An Unknown Early Panel by Pieter Bruegel the Elder," *Burlington Magazine*, XCVII, 1955, p. 240).

[26] Illus., for example, in E. Panofsky, *Early Netherlandish Painting*, II, 1953, fig. 90. Prof.

Herbert Kessler has pointed out to me that the drawing of the ploughman is different in the March miniature of the *Grimani Breviary*, whose calendar pictures adapt those of the Chantilly *Hours*, and thus this most sumptuous product of the Bruges-Ghent school of illumination at the time of Patinir would not have served as model.

and was in her library at Malines, where it would surely have been seen by Dürer when he was shown her treasures in 1521. The March miniature would have been studied a few years earlier either by Patinir himself, or by another artist who would have provided him with a drawing of the ploughman. Two accessories to the Holy Family group were taken with little change from compositions created by Gerard David: the grazing ass, and the wicker travel basket. Of the basket Patinir makes a still life by adding white saddle bags and the walking stick of Joseph; and this group of objects is repeated, sometimes with the addition of a water gourd, in every other composition of the theme by Patinir and his workshop.[27] As in the David scheme, Joseph is always in the distance, in order not to detract from the inherent power of a Madonna image. He performs his fatherly tasks either by dipping water from the miraculous spring, fetching a pot of porridge, or gathering fruit from a tree.[28]

Probably as a prelude to the theatrical Kaufmann-Kaus Triptych, though painted at about the same time (ca. 1515-16), Patinir undertook what was to remain his least narrative, most restrained and peaceful composition of the *Rest on the Flight*, today in the Thyssen Collection in Lugano (Fig. 12). It is compositionally allied in mirror image to the landscape with the preaching of the Baptist (Fig. 10): a rocky middle distance (here with farmhouse and castle) on one side, while the other opens to an endless vista consisting of a winding river, gently rolling fields and forests, and distant hills. It is curious that this unspectacular landscape was copied by Patinir's workshop more often than any other, and that it greatly appealed to Joos van Cleve. The Madonna is now immersed in a locale that offers no threat. Far behind her Joseph gathers fruit from a sheltering grove, while the ass grazes in distant isolation at the left.

Critical opinion of the picture has been at variance. As long ago as 1902 Hulin de Loo attributed it to Patinir and wrote of the fine state of preservation of the surface, except for the face of the Madonna, which was somewhat abraded.[29] Baldass places it very early in Patinir's career because of what he feels to be the influence not only of David but of Memling (in the vista at the left); while Hoogewerff believes

[27] An opened basket and gourd appear in the earliest of David's four variants of his *Rest on the Flight*, the one in Lisbon (in accordance with the chronology established by L. Baldass in "G. David als Landschaftsmaler," Vienna *Jahrbuch*, NF X, 1936, p. 93 and abb. 59). The closed basket alone appears in the variants in the Prado and National Gallery, Washington (Friedländer, VI, nos. 212 and 214).

[28] The motif of Joseph picking or gathering fruit appears in many German and Netherlandish compositions of the 15th and 16th centuries; for Patinir the inspiration may have

been, again, David's *Rest* (Lisbon).

The textual source for the palm tree which bent at the command of the Child to offer its fruit was Pseudo-Matthew, Ch. XX. The same text relates the story of the miraculous spring. Though the spring is always shown, the palm tree was apparently never adopted by Patinir. It does occur in the following paintings by the Master of the Half-Lengths or his workshop: Vienna *Rest*, Fig. 79; Raleigh *Flight*, Fig. 81; and Basel *Rest*, Fig. 91.

[29] *Catalogue critique*, p. 54.

it to be the work of a pupil and suggests Joos van Cleve.[30] This last opinion is based, wrongly we believe, on the fact that Joos adapts this landscape for a picture of his own, a *Rest on the Flight* today in Brussels (Fig. 14). In this composition an unusually fine figure of the nursing Madonna was so esteemed that it was copied in turn in paintings produced by the Patinir workshop. There can be no doubt that the workshops of Joos and Patinir were closely connected in Antwerp, a point to be discussed in the next chapter. The painting in Lugano, I feel, is a thoroughly characteristic work by Patinir himself in his early middle period.

It is rather surprising to discover that Patinir, whose main concern was with landscape, occasionally brought iconographical innovations to time-honored themes. There are several novelties in the comparatively small, multi-scene panel which features the *Assumption of the Virgin* (Johnson Collection, Philadelphia) (Fig. 20). The painting bears the coat of arms of Lucas Rem in the lower right-hand corner (Fig. 25); and as I have suggested, it was probably commissioned from Patinir in Antwerp in 1516-17. This explains the presence of Luke, name saint of Lucas Rem, and of Luke's symbol the ox (or bull) as tiny grisaille figures flanking the roundel Ascension of Christ in the upper right corner (Fig. 24). The grisailles in the corresponding spaces opposite, adjoining the roundel of the night Nativity (or *Christnacht*)[31] depict a pilgrim with staff and rosary, and an angel displaying the traditional symbol of the pilgrim, a scallop shell (Fig. 22). Appropriate for the pious Rem, who was much addicted to pilgrimages, the saint might be the archetypal pilgrim James himself, or else quite possibly Jost (or Jodok), the adopted saint of Pilgrims to Compostella.[32] The two other scenes in grisaille in the spandrels above the carved, rounded arch of the inner frame are the Adoration of the Magi and the Ascension of Christ.

The story of the burial of the Virgin Mary is rare in Flemish painting, and seemingly only Albert Bouts's well-known triptych of the *Assumption* (Brussels) offers a precedent for Patinir.[33] The Apostles in the foreground are grouped about Mary's grave site (an open sarcophagus in Bouts), as she is borne aloft by angels to the Trinity above. In tiny scale in the landscape background is the funeral procession that preceded the entombment in the Biblical valley of Jehosaphat, outside the walls of Jerusalem. Apparently unique in Western painting is the idea of a low-

---

[30] Baldass, 1918, p. 114; Hoogewerff, 1954, pp. 25-26.

[31] On the origin in the milieu of Hugo van der Goes of the *Christnacht*, a special type of adoration of the Newborn as a night scene, see F. Winkler, *Hugo van der Goes*, Berlin, 1964, pp. 141-54. Patinir's spacious inscenation brings to mind the compositions of Bosch and Altdorfer.

[32] Among the misfortunes against which St. Jost gave protection was that of storms at sea; thus he would be a most appropriate saint for Rem, whose fortune depended upon the safe transit of ships (see K. Künstle, *Ikonographie der christlichen Kunst*, Freiburg, 1926, II, pp. 330-31).

[33] M. Wéra, "Contribution à l'étude d'Albert Bouts," *Revue Belge . . .*, XX, 1951, pp. 139-44.

lying cave to shelter the sarcophagus. This is mentioned in apocryphal literature, together with the legend that Mary had dropped her girdle to Thomas as she ascended. In Patinir's composition Thomas is shown as the dark-bearded figure entering the cave, holding what appears to be a rosary along with the girdle.[34] Another innovation is the depiction of a bonfire behind the procession in the middle distance, probably inspired by Voragine's account in the *Golden Legend*, "Jews incited each other to kill the disciples and burn the body which had borne the imposter."[35] God the Father and the Son sit on a throne of blue and gold, awaiting with opened arms the uncrowned Queen of Heaven, who is garbed in the dark and light blue robes which denote her persevering faith to the end. Mary is raised in prayerful majesty by seven angels who open her mantle so that she is displayed in her aspect as Madonna of Mercy, while a host of other angels, clad in pink and blue, adore her.[36]

In the sweep of the low-lying landscape across the breadth of the composition and back to the sprawling port city of Jerusalem the picture gives us, in Patinir's middle period, a forecast of the world landscape that will characterize his late works. The style of the figures and drapery is very characteristic of the Master and will be discussed in Chapter III.

Perhaps next in chronological order is a painting that nicely reveals all of the characteristics of this half-way point in the career of the painter. About four and a half feet in width, *Landscape with St. Jerome* (Louvre) is Patinir's largest composition of an interrelated group depicting this scene (Fig. 26). The disposition of landscape and staffage is similar to the Lugano *Rest*, though now in the place of a tranquil grove of trees there are rugged, mountainous rocks to indicate the rigor of Jerome's life in the wilderness. The spindling tree in the foreground is repeated to convey a sense of scale. On the left is a similar though more detailed river valley landscape, while nestled in the mountains on the right is a splendid Gothic-Romanesque church, the monastery of Jerome. A tiny group of figures and animals is barely

---

[34] The idea of the cave, and the arrival of Thomas at the tomb with the girdle that he had received on the Mount of Olives, is based upon the apocryphal story of John the Theologian (A. Roberts and J. Donaldson, *The Ante-Nicene Fathers*, VIII, N.Y., 1903, pp. 592-94). When the rare theme of Thomas and the Girdle are undertaken at all in the North, as on the left wing of the Triptych by Albert Bouts, the Apostle is shown receiving it from a messenger angel. This exclusively Northern European motif may have had its genesis in Petrus Christus' *Death of the Virgin*, now in the National Gallery, Washington (see Jonathan Brown, "Dos Obras

Tempranas de Bartolome Bermejo y su Relacion con Flandes," *Archivo Español de Arte*, 36, 1963, pp. 269-79).

[35] Quoted in Y. Hirn, *The Sacred Shrine*, London, 1958 (rev. ed.), p. 297.

[36] There are compositional similarities between Patinir's and Miguel Sithium's famous little picture of the *Assumption of the Virgin*, painted ca. 1500 for Queen Isabella of Spain. Identified by M. J. Friedländer (in *Cicerone*, 1929, pp. 249ff.), the painting was acquired in 1965 by the National Gallery in Washington. During Patinir's lifetime it was in the collection of Margaret of Austria at Malines.

discernible in the churchyard. Here Jerome appears in the denouement of the story of the theft of the monastery ass, as related in Voragine's *Golden Legend*.[37] Merchants, traveling with camels, had stolen the ass that Jerome's pet lion had been entrusted to guard. Recognizing the thieves as they returned one day by the same route, the lion pounced upon the caravan, shown here in the middle distance before a tunnel through the rocks. With the ass safely returned, the Saint forgives both lion and merchants.

In the central foreground Jerome kneels with book, scourge, and flagellant's stone in a rude shelter before the rocks, praying before a crucifix. An aged, white-bearded, barefoot ascetic, he has cast aside those vanity symbols which attested his churchly eminence, the red cardinal's robe and hat, and thrown them upon the jagged stump of a dead tree. This idea may well have been derived from a composition by Bosch, now in the Museum of Fine Arts in Ghent.[38] Many animals join the usual rabbits and mountain goat, favorites of Patinir: a flock of sheep and a nearly complete inventory of beasts of burden in the distant world of the farmer. Jerome is surrounded with fauna symbolizing man's struggle with good and evil, of temptation and redemption: doves and owl, salamanders and parrot. Quite in the spirit of Bosch, for whom it was almost an emblem, the owl has a double meaning. It was a reference to the great wisdom of the Saint, but at the same time it was a sign of the presence of the Tempter—both aspects emphasized by the hidden position of the owl in a hollow in the rock above Jerome.[39] The salamanders by the foreground spring would have conveyed to the knowledgeable viewer of the time the good Christian's constancy in the face of adversity, but at the same time the salamander was believed to poison fruit trees as well as springs, and like the owl could be a sign of the presence of the Tempter.[40] On the edge of the rocks behind Jerome a dove-cote is attached to a cliff dwelling, while at the extreme left boundary of the picture a dog chases white doves. Quite possibly here the dove is symbolic of the temptations of sensual pleasure, which Jerome records plagued him in the wilderness.[41] Also perhaps the parrot on the roof of the hut symbolically joins the forces of redemption, standing for the Redeemer himself. Held by the child in Jan van Eyck's *Madonna with Canon van der Paele* (Bruges), the parrot alone of animals was capable of speech and hence was identified with the *Logos*.[42]

[37] Jacopo da Voragine, *The Golden Legend* (tr. G. Ryan and H. Ripperger), New York, 1941, II, pp. 587ff.

[38] Illus. in L. Baldass, *H. Bosch*, New York, 1960, pl. 77.

[39] Both owl and salamander are present in Bosch's painting in Ghent. On the meaning of the owl see L. Charbonneau-Lassay, *Le bestiaire du Christ*, Bruges, 1940, pp. 461-70.

[40] *Ibid.*, pp. 815-18; R. A. Koch, "The Salamander in Van der Goes' Garden of Eden," *Warburg Journal*, XXVIII, 1965, pp. 323-26.

[41] Voragine, ed. cit., II, p. 589.

[42] On the parrot as a *Logos* symbol see G. Marlier, *Ambrosius Benson*, Damme, 1957, p. 111. In the *Paele Madonna* the Christ Child also holds flowers, possibly as an illusion to the Song of Solomon, 2: 1: "I am the flower of the

A lackluster workshop copy of this painting (Venice, Ca d'Oro) (Fig. 27) was much reduced in both size and in details, for purchase by the economy-minded Lucas Rem, and all of these symbolic animals are omitted. Added however to the middle-distant landscape at the left are the figures of a farmer with harrow, a sower of grain, and a blind man being led by a youth. These details have been interpolated from later compositions by Patinir, and we are thereby able to give an approximate date to this workshop copy.[43]

The Prado *Landscape with Saint Jerome* (Fig. 28) is one of the larger masterworks (three feet in breadth) and is Patinir's most spectacular interpretation of the subject. It was a fitting later acquisition by Philip II, for it became a cult picture of the chapter of the Hieronymite Order which he had established in the Escorial. As in the early composition with the martyrdom of St. Catherine, the high eye level permits an extensive sweep of landscape which rises nearly to the top frame of the picture. Jagged rocks protect the open mud-and-wattle shelter of Jerome in the foreground, while rock fingers, like giant crystals, stab the sky in a distant corner of the picture. It is the artist's most daringly unbalanced—or rather dynamically balanced—composition, fulfilling on the surface of a large panel a propensity manifested in his early style. The monastic establishment of the Saint is repeated from the picture in the Louvre with very few changes; however it is now placed on a high promontory, at an uncertain distance behind the rocks of the foreground. This spatial ambiguity, along with other pictorial elements, lends a vaguely romantic mood to the picture: the brightly lighted tunnel which opens in the rock behind Jerome, the dark clouds silhouetting ghostly mountains that no man could scale, and the storm at sea. The Saint has now put aside his devotional aids—crucifix, book, and skull—[44]while he removes a thorn from the lion's paw.[45] Nearby, a rabbit munches what little has been provided for forage, while the dead tree again not only enhances the idea of barren wilderness but gives scale to the figure without blocking the distant view, as would a tree with foliage. Further on, a blind man is about to be led by a boy across a rustic bridge. This touch of pathos need not be pure genre, for Jerome had

---

field and the lily of the valleys." See R. A. Koch, "Flower Symbolism in the Portinari Altar," *Art Bulletin*, XLVI, 1964, p. 71.

There is another possible meaning. Like the goldfinch, the parrot can be associated with the classical *charadrius*, a bird which healed a sick man by looking at him, drawing the illness into himself (H. Friedmann, *The Symbolic Goldfinch*, New York, 1946, pp. 10ff., 54-55).

[43] Rem's acquisition was made after his marriage, probably when he was in Antwerp in 1520. See Chapter I, p. 11.

[44] The skull, an established element in Italian portrayals of the penitent Jerome was apparently associated with the Saint in the North for the first time in Dürer's 1514 engraving of Jerome in his Cell. It is given great importance in the famous *memento mori* painting of Jerome (Lisbon) that Dürer painted in Antwerp in 1521 (H. W. Janson, "The Putto with the Death's Head," *Art Bulletin*, XIX, 1937, pp. 430-31).

[45] See G. Ring, "St. Jerome Extracting the Thorn from the Lion's Foot," *Art Bulletin*, XXVII, 1945, pp. 188ff.

come to be regarded as patron of those with eye trouble, an appropriate honor for the great scholar.[46] Far away, beneath the storm clouds by the distant shore, the camel caravan approaches, while near the foreground at the right it is surprised by the lion. The scene of forgiveness again takes place before the monastery, the finale of a cinematic narrative.

There is strong evidence that Patinir himself made a small variant composition of the Prado *Jerome*. In it he retained with little change in drawing the theme of Jerome extracting the thorn, the design of the near- and far-distant rock masses, and all of the far-distant landscape at the right. Of the changes, a major compositional one was made whereby the landscape was extended on the left, giving a more spacious setting to the distant mountains. In the foothills are a castle and a pagan temple with its outdoor idol. Patinir improves upon the scale of the monastic establishment on the plateau by redesigning it as a simple Romanesque church; he dispenses with the attributes of Jerome; and in the lower right corner he reinterprets Voragine's story by depicting monks chopping wood, while the lion sleeps and the ass is stolen. Though the hypothetical original has apparently not survived, there are several copies of this variant composition. The best is of sufficiently fine quality to be by Patinir himself, the well-known picture in the National Gallery, London, which consists of just the left half of the composition (Fig. 30). Uncut at the right and hence not a fragment, this little gem makes a self-sufficient and dramatic landscape study of rocks and angry sky. The palette is harmoniously cool, forming beautiful transitions from a brownish-green foreground through rocks that are first slate gray and then blue-white, crowned above by blue clouds of deep intensity. Two further copies of the entire composition, one today in Wuppertal-Elberfeld (Fig. 31) and the other in Zurich (Fig. 75), are also small, each just under fourteen inches in width. Neither, I believe, was made by Patinir himself, notwithstanding Friedländer's curious decision that both are by Patinir (along with the London painting) and are "replicas of equal quality."[47] The Wuppertal-Elberfeld painting is spiritless and technically weak; while the Zurich picture, I feel, bears the unmistakable style and iconographical traits of the Master of the Half-Lengths. I should like to propose a lost original variant by Patinir of the Prado *Jerome* which he himself then copied in the abbreviated composition in London, and of which his workshop made the copy in Wuppertal-Elberfeld along with an adaptation of the composition in a triptych now in Palermo (Fig. 36).[48] The Zurich copy was made by the Master of the Half-Lengths, painting his earliest known landscape, possibly as a pupil of Patinir. This and his other landscape paintings are the subject of Chapter IV.

[46] L. Réau, *Iconographie de l'art chrétien*, Paris, 1958, III, Pt. 2, p. 742.

[47] IX, p. 158, no. 243a and b.

[48] It is difficult to decide whether the larger and more splendid Prado composition was painted first, or the lost version. It is easy to rationalize either viewpoint. They may well have been painted nearly simultaneously.

The Zurich picture is one of a pair of paintings that are practically identical in size and compatible in both composition and subject matter. Though perceptibly different in style, they seem to have survived together as a pair.[49] The other represents a female counterpart to St. Jerome, St. Mary Magdalene, who also led for a while the life of a penitent in the wilderness. Though its subject has often been misinterpreted, the picture should properly bear the title "Landscape with Ecstasy of Mary Magdalene" (Fig. 32). Later mediaeval legend held that the Magdalene spent the last years of her life as a hermit in a mountain cave near the Southern coast of France, a site called la Sainte-Baume. The *Golden Legend* records that every day, at each of the canonical hours of prayer, angels bore her aloft in ecstasy as she "heard the glorious chants of the heavenly hosts"; and this is the scene given by Patinir in tiny scale, high above the floor of the grotto.[50] La Sainte-Baume became a famous pilgrimage site, visited by kings and commoners (including Lucas Rem), and it so remains to this day. Most remarkable is the fact that Patinir represents the actual site, in a very stylized manner of course, as it appeared in his own day, complete with hostelry, shrine, and pilgrims. He would have known it either by means of a trip to la Sainte-Baume[51]—a journey for which there is otherwise no valid evidence—or more probably through a drawing brought to Antwerp by a friend. Soon afterwards, Patinir himself again uses the profile of the famous mountain as a picturesque rock motif in the Berlin *Rest on the Flight* (Fig. 40); and it is adopted by a number of other painters of the Antwerp school in the first half of the sixteenth century, among them Herri met de Bles in a fine little picture today in Berlin (Fig. 33).[52]

The Zurich *Magdalene* seems a shade too weak in execution to be by the hand of Patinir himself, and logic suggests that it was painted by the Master of the Half-Lengths as a companion piece to his copy of the *Jerome*. If true, he completely submerged his own personality in a close and rather dry copy. It is clear in any case that the Patinir originals were together in his studio, for his workshop combined the two compositions in at least two other paintings. The Palermo Triptych (Fig. 36) features the Zurich Jerome composition in the central panel and left wing, while the Magdalene landscape is adapted as the background of the right wing. The second picture is a small roundel now in the Mayer van den Bergh Museum in Antwerp (Fig. 34), wherein the foreground rocks of Jerome are combined with the mountain of the Magdelene as the site for his monastery.

The iconographic scheme of the foreground of the Palermo Triptych (SS.

[49] They were together in the Chiesa Collection, sold in 1925, and have so remained to the present.

[50] Ed. cited, II, pp. 360-61.

[51] G. J. Hoogewerff, "Joachim Patenier en Italie," *Revue d'art*, XLV, 1928, pp. 117-34.

[52] R. A. Koch, "La Sainte-Baume in Flemish Landscape Painting of the Sixteenth Century," *G.d.B.-A.*, LXVI, 1965, pp. 273-82.

Jerome and Anthony, and the Baptism of Christ) had probably been suggested by the Master's finest altarpiece, the Metropolitan Museum's *Triptych with Penitence of Jerome* (Fig. 35). Prominent in the foreground of the central panel, a Jerome of greater seriousness than before—and hence suited to devotional purposes as a church altarpiece—beats his breast as he kneels in the wilderness. On the left wing is the Baptism of Christ, a rather ineffective compression in a narrow space of the theme of Patinir's earlier treatment (Fig. 8). Above the figures, the dove is sent down by God the Father, who superintends from the clouds above; and John again preaches in the distance. On the right wing sits a sallow-skinned St. Anthony, his meditations interrupted as he is beset by Boschian creatures. Included are a tiny owl on a dead branch, and a half-hidden, enigmatic "portrait" of a young man. Far away, near the shore of a bay, is the visit of Anthony with the anchorite St. Paul, tiny figures seated on a bench before a country chapel.

A single high horizon line unites the broad world landscape which spreads in unprecedented grandeur across the triptych. As in the Prado *Jerome* a dynamic balance of landscape elements is effected, with a distant rock mass uniting the left wing and central panel in opposition to a broad expanse of land and water which joins the center with the right wing. Thus Patinir formally brings together in brotherhood these three exemplars of the ascetic Christian life, however much they were separated in historical time. On the exterior of the altarpiece, which like the interior is in an excellent state of preservation, are the grisaille figures of St. Sebald and the group of St. Anne with the Madonna and Child (Fig. 38).

A pious worshiper kneeling before this altarpiece could easily have his mind distracted by a landscape filled with details: people roaming the countryside like ants, singly and in pairs; a couple milking a cow beneath a palm tree in the distance on the left wing; and hounds pursuing a stag across the bright yellow-green fields in the central panel. Beyond a windmill, on the lake beside a chateau, are swans, monstrously out of scale in order that they may be seen. Near the foreground Patinir finally makes clearly visible the episode of Jerome's forgiveness of the merchantmen, though it necessitates a division of the monastery structures. The scene with the two kneeling traders, the Saint, lion, ass, and a pair of camels is witnessed by a peacock in full feather, a symbol of "the perfect man, just and holy, who is not corrupted by any vice."[53] A crucifix and scourge rest on the ground before Jerome, as in the Louvre composition, though now his penitence is more physical. A goldfinch perches nearby as a symbol of the redemptive powers of Christ, while to the left of the Saint is another emblem of redemption, the tree half-dead, half-alive.[54] Yet another is the

[53] Charbonneau-Lassay, *op.cit.*, pp. 624-26.
[54] On the meaning of the goldfinch see above, n. 43; on the meaning of the tree see M. R. Bennett, "The Legend of the Green Tree and the Dry," *Archaeological Journal*, LXXXIII, 1926, pp. 21-32.

symbolism of the salamander in juxtaposition with a piece of red coral, the latter a well-known mediaeval antidote to the devil and thus to the temptation represented by the salamander.[55] Among the thick, Campin-like carpet of plants by the tree stump that has sprung to new life is a dandelion, strawberry in flower and fruit, plantain, and thistle—all painted with utmost verisimilitude in tribute to the Creator whose works they evoked.[56] Patinir's continuation of the use of disguised natural symbols to such a degree is rather surprising in view of the fact that except for time-honored ones they had ceased to be a matter of preoccupation with Netherlandish artists after the time of Hugo van der Goes in the 1470's. This may be partly accounted for in that Patinir's "return to nature" was in a sense a latter-day experiencing of the "discovery of nature" by the earlier Flemish masters of the first half of the fifteenth century.

When Patinir returns to the theme of the *Rest on the Flight* with the fine painting now in Berlin (Fig. 40), he forsakes the compositional idea of the Lugano picture, in which the subject was mainly a foil for the landscape, and he takes up again a monumental presentation of the Madonna. It is interesting to note that now for the first time of which we may be certain, Patinir enlists the services of another artist, Joos van Cleve, to paint the figures of the Virgin and Child. Van Cleve was a noted painter of figures, especially Madonnas, and of portraits, as was Quentin Massys. It is to both of these colleagues and friends in the Antwerp Guild that Patinir turns for collaboration, relatively late in his career.

As in no other composition Patinir assembles detail after detail, in his customarily orderly fashion, to form an epic world landscape. Now there are neither rocks nor trees on either side to arrest the eye and block the view. There is a fine unity of near and distant elements in the strong and solidly constructed central axis, which is comprised of the Madonna, the still life of travel baggage from the Kaufmann-Kaus Triptych (to which a goldfinch has been added), and a tree in full leafage. The axis continues on a winding road behind Mary to the monumental rock formation, a paraphrase of the site of la Sainte-Baume, with its peak now disappearing in the clouds. The Mother of God is placed unprotected on an open hill in the foreground, her safety in a peaceful nature underscored by the birds and a deer in a nearby glade. A modest fire with its cooking pot gives warmth to Mary and the naked Child, whose attention is diverted by a thrush-like bird that has perched nearby. Beside the miraculous spring is the yellow iris, thistle, and again a dead tree that has come to life again, with its possible allusion to the redemptive power of the Saviour. Completely absorbed in the populous landscape are the story-telling episodes of the Massacre of the Innocents and the Miraculous Wheatfield; and one must also look closely to

---

[55] Charbonneau-Lassay, *op.cit.*, p. 941; and the author's article cited in n. 40 above.

[56] L. Behling, *Die Pflanze in der mittelalterlichen Tafelmalerei*, Weimar, 1957, passim.

find Joseph, who is leading the ass along a road in the country village at the left, as well as the toppling idol, which is on the axis above the head of Mary. In the far distance is a large port city that is vaguely reminiscent of Antwerp. There is little in fact in this exciting panorama that would have been alien to a contemporary of Patinir who traveled between the Rivers Scheldt and Meuse with open eyes.

LATE PERIOD

It is fitting that a royal collector, Philip II, somehow managed to acquire every one of the four masterworks by Patinir that may be ascribed, for stylistic reasons, to the Master's late period. This may be said to comprise the last three or four years of a career which we have reason to believe was prematurely ended in 1524, as discussed in the first chapter. The paintings are the *Rest on the Flight* (Fig. 39), *Temptation of St. Anthony* (Fig. 44), and *Landscape with Charon's Boat* (Fig. 54), all today in the Prado, and the *St. Christopher* (Fig. 49), which has remained in the Escorial. One reason for Philip's interest may well have been the fact that in all four of these grandiose compositions the countryside has been "demonized in the spirit of Bosch,"[57] and thus they catered to the morbid proclivity of the Monarch. Patinir's interest in the style and iconography of Bosch now comes to fruition. His draughtsmanship remains precise and even finicking to the end, but details are better integrated and the transition between foreground and distant horizon is more deftly realized. Except for the *Rest on the Flight* the farthermost distance is now conceived as a nearly unbroken stretch across the entire composition. It would be wrong to call his late technique "painterly," despite a much greater assurance in the nuance of light and shadow in the far distance, best seen in the mountains and stunning cloud structure of the painting with Christopher. The general effect of the last three landscapes is one of infinite expanse, suitable stages for myriad details and actions that contrast peace and terror, salvation and violence.

The order in which the pictures of the late period came into being is of little matter since they form a homogeneous group; but as the *Rest on the Flight* (Fig. 39) bears more of the traits of the late middle period we shall consider it first. The monumental figure of the Madonna, robed in dazzling bluish-white and nursing the Child, is closely connected with the style of Quentin Massys and thus presents a problem that will be discussed in Chapter III. The worldly possessions of the Holy Family have now been given compositional prominence at the feet of Mary, in the immediate foreground. To this still life a water gourd with stopper has been added; and it is of interest to note that the wicker basket is viewed from an angle that Patinir elects never to change. The vine that clings to the nearer of two fruited trees may,

[57] Friedländer, IX, p. 110.

37

because of its prominence, have been intended to evoke Christ's words, "I am the Vine" (Fig. 42).[58] They are part of a veritable botanical garden that the artist creates in the foreground, as though to show nature rejoicing at the danger passed—or almost passed; for at the edge of the deep woods a crossbowman prepares to load his weapon, arrow in mouth. A very similar one appears in Dürer's woodcut print, made in 1503, of the Martyrdom of St. Sebastian; and this may well have been the source for Patinir. Mary is seated on a rise of ground, with rounded folds of earth and receding tree-trunks measuring, as in a park, the space behind her.

Joseph emerges with a cooking pot from a valley at the left, while in the land-scape behind him is the favorite motif of an archway and pair of travelers (Fig. 42). Their road leads to the most interesting of the Master's architectural fantasies: a rounded, Romanesque-Gothic temple. From its campanile two idols topple, as the sacrifice of a goose is about to be made before a snouted creature seated upon an altar. This is again a reference, and a very picturesque one, to the fall of the idols and the Egyptian temple of Heliopolis, as mentioned in the *Golden Legend*;[59] and the motif of the pagan offering is an adaptation from Bosch's *Triptych of St. Anthony* in Lisbon.[60]

The splendid wheatfield scene at the right (Fig. 43) is an emendation of the one in the Kaufmann-Kaus Triptych, where it appears as a vignette more or less detached from the foreground (Fig. 16). Now Patinir imparts both rhythm and better scale to the composition by the introduction of a grove of trees to echo, in a reversed direction, the group in the foreground. The "Chantilly" ploughman has been dropped, and in his place the farmer with the horse-drawn harrow has been re-oriented parallel to the picture plane. A flock of chickens gobbles the grain that is being broadcast by a sower, an addition to the scene which underscores the miracle of the adjacent field of grain that has ripened out of season. Two other details bring to life the far edge of the field: a sow suckles her young, while a squatting man relieves himself.[61] The donkey of the Holy Family is tethered near what was once another pagan idol, now reduced to a pair of feet upon a ball stone pedestal. In a rather startling contrast to the mottled earth colors that play across the landscape, the artist has made of the newly ploughed field an unmodulated patch of purple; and so color, as well as detail, plays a role in this composition in drawing the viewer's

[58] This appears to be a grapevine, though it is without fruit. In art a grapevine, normally fruited, symbolized the sacrifice of Christ. Giovanni Bellini similarly had represented a fruitless vine in the *St. Francis* in the Frick Collection, and Millard Meiss observes that the absence of grapes seems pointed (*Giovanni Bellini's St. Francis in the Frick Collection*, Princeton, 1964, p. 23).

[59] Ed. cited, I, p. 66.

[60] It occurs as part of the decoration on the central building (illus. in Baldass, *H. Bosch*, 1960, pl. 97).

[61] For Van Mander's account of this detail see above, Chapter I, p. 8.

eye to the middle distance. For once, late in his career, Patinir nearly abandons his abiding interest in the far away surface of the earth.

The *Temptation of St. Anthony*, painted in collaboration with Quentin Massys, is grandly conceived and huge in size, five feet in height and nearly six feet in breadth (Fig. 44). It is a not unworthy companion to Bosch's great treatment of the theme in the Lisbon triptych; but whereas Bosch produced a poetic fantasy of incredible inspiration, Patinir and Massys remain earth-bound and literal. There were no fewer than five episodes in the tribulations of St. Anthony, as recorded in popular literature by Voragine,[62] and all have been included in this composition. First, the hermit was attacked by demons in the form of wild beasts, when he was in an "Egyptian tomb." This is shown, in the middle distance at the center, as a group of rude shelters, the elevated one ablaze. Anthony's hair is also on fire as he attempts to flee, only to fall prostrate before the assault of a snake, toad, a leprous character, and even his own attribute, a pig.[63] At the same time an army of ominous creatures approaches over the hill. The second tribulation is the often depicted airborne one, where he is assaulted by demons in an excruciating test of his faith. As in the painting by Bosch, a helmeted beast rides a bloated fish, an image conceivably inspired by Voragine's remark, "Just as fish die when they come out of water, so do monks lose their peace when they leave their cell."[64] After these trials, an exhausted Anthony lies on the ground, in the middle-distant landscape. He is being addressed by Christ, who assures him that all the while He was present.[65] The remaining two episodes tell of the Saint's temptations. In the foreground is Massys' memorable interpretation of the hermit as a well-groomed, almost courtly gentleman (Fig. 45). About his head are the light rays of sanctification, for he refuses the apple of evil and the blandishments of three beautifully attired temptresses. They are goaded by a "procuress" whose ugly features and headdress recall the so-called "Ugly Duchess" of Massys (London, National Gallery). While his rosary with its shell lies useless on the ground, near a blossoming thistle, Anthony is tugged at by a monkey, another of the Devil's agents. The clothed "ladies" fail; and so does a second group of half-naked females in the distance at the right (Fig. 46). They tempt him both with their flesh and with drink, at an insidious boating party. Water jug in hand, the resolute Saint makes a gesture of exorcism as he leaves the scene.

Finally, Anthony is permitted to meditate quietly on a bench outside his chapel,

[62] Ed. cit., I, pp. 99ff.

[63] The pig was an allusion to Anthony's patronage of swine-breeders, for its lard was deemed effective against the fungus disease which we call erysipelas but which was then known as "St. Anthony's fire." The Saint, himself afire, is surely meant to be an allusion to this disease.

[64] Ed. cit., I, p. 101.

[65] The reader is reminded of the colloquy between Christ and Anthony as written in the corner of Grünewald's composition of the torment of the Saint on the Isenheim Altar (Colmar). Recorded by Voragine, Anthony's complaint, and not Christ's reassuring answer, is the only part lettered by Grünewald.

which Patinir has placed on a middle-distant promontory at the left (Fig. 47). Like the monastery of Jerome, in the Prado composition, the building is placed before a symbolically cloud-darkened, mountainous wilderness; but now the entire country-side is cast in shadow, while human activity continues in the harbor town in the center, and in the village and fields at the right, where a shepherd tends his flocks. Always for the good Christian who resists evil, there is the luminous horizon of hope, of another day and a glorious eternity.

A large woodcut of the Temptation of St. Anthony bears the date 1522 (Fig. 48). It has been attributed to Jan Wellens de Cock, older colleague of Patinir in the Antwerp painters' guild between 1503 and his death in 1526.[66] The design contains details which suggest familiarity with the Patinir-Massys composition, namely the inclusion and relative positioning of all four of the subsidiary actions, as well as the adaptation of the Massys "procuress." We may thus be entitled to assume a date of 1522, or shortly before, for the painting.

Along with Anthony one of the more popular of the fourteen Auxiliary Saints, the giant Christopher was the patron of travelers and was invoked principally against sudden and brutal death. Christopher was a natural subject for artists interested in landscape painting; and for this reason Bouts and his school, Bosch, Jan Wellens de Cock, and Patinir and his followers were drawn to the theme more than once. Of all of their interpretations, the painting by Patinir now in the Escorial is easily the most memorable because of its unusual size—about four feet in breadth—the vastness of its setting, its multitude of interesting details, and its mood (Fig. 49).

As Voragine relates the story, it was an aged hermit who had taught Christopher about the Saviour.[67] Patinir includes him at the left, dressed in a dark blue robe, his frailty emphasized by his need of a cane and a tree-trunk for support (Fig. 51). The hut behind the hermit has been conceived as a ruinous tree-house fantasy, like the place of torture of St. Anthony. Both the concept and certain details derive from Bosch: an inverted pot, a snarling dog, and a sinister, semi-dressed man drying a garment before a fire in the darkened ground floor. Outside, a pilgrim kneels before a shrine, praying before the statue of a Madonna and a crucifix—that potent image which so frightened the Devil that Christopher had been led to abandon his pagan faith; and at the same time an allusion is made to the fact that the hermit first taught

---

[66] Friedländer, XI, taf. XLVI. Formerly thought to be by Bosch, the woodcut was first attributed to Jan Wellens de Cock by M. J. Friedländer ("Jan Wellens de Cock," *Z.f.b.K*, NF 1917/18, pp. 67ff.; see also Hollstein, *Dutch and Flemish Etchings . . .* , IV, n.d. [1951], p. 192).

Jan de Cock (along with Joos van Cleve) was a dean of the Antwerp guild in 1520, and hence would have been a friend of Patinir. His paintings of Jerome, Christopher, Anthony, and of Lot and his Daughters, all in landscape settings, are much more mannered in style than Patinir's, but they bear a certain relationship to them (cf. Friedländer, XI, pls. XLV-LI).

[67] Ed. cit., II, pp. 377-82.

Christopher "how to pray" (Voragine). Many other details possess overtones of disaster or violence. On the near-distant shore a dead body is being fished ashore by two monks. Tied to a board and with a slip of paper at his waist, the corpse is explainable perhaps as an indication of foul play—a less lucky Jonah—and of the dangers of the water.[68] A fiery catastrophe has overtaken the seaport town in the far distance, while in its main square is a scene of mob violence (Fig. 52). Armies on foot and horseback, very reminiscent of those in Bosch's *Adoration of the Magi* (Prado), probably illustrate, as they pillage the countryside, the episode in Voragine in which two hundred soldiers seek out Christopher to take him back to the city. Evil has become so prevalent in this melancholy landscape that two merchant ships are locked in conflict at the entrance to the harbor. On the road which winds along the river bank at the right, rendered in fine perspective, is a pair of those travelers who are rarely absent from a Patinir composition; while nearby two men wash themselves as they await transportation across the river.[69] As in several earlier compositions of the artist, the river is foreshortened to lead back directly from the foreground, an old technique in Flemish painting that Patinir now exploits with great effect. Deep blue-green water silhouettes the Saint, who wears a bluish-white robe with tan trousers rolled to the knee, trailing in the water a deep red mantle. Watery gray clouds fill much of the sky, while black birds, symbolizing death, wheel about in the sky in the compositional area behind the dead tree. In the foreground is the Master's most prominent treatment of the evil salamander, while the usual yellow-white iris and a strawberry plant lend one of the few notes of relief to this vast and desolate picture of unholiness and the sorry state into which mankind had fallen.

Related to this painting is a much smaller composition, today in a private collection in Switzerland, as far as I know, that may have come from the Patinir workshop (Fig. 53). Lacking the landscape sweep and most of the interesting detail of its model, this near night scene has a novelty which deserves comment. The conventional crystal orb of Earth held by the Child in the Escorial painting becomes a huge, luminous bluish-grey sphere which rests on the Giant's back, seeming to reflect in mirror image reduction the river landscape of the composition itself. This landscape within a landscape, reminiscent of Bosch, nicely illustrates Christ's words to Christopher, as transmitted by the *Golden Legend*: "Do not be surprised. . . . You have borne not only the world on your shoulders but He who has created the world."[70]

Patinir's most remarkable composition has been variously called "The Underworld," "Heaven and Hell," "The River Styx," and "Charon." I suggest "Landscape

---

[68] On this theme see G. Glück, "Pieter Bruegel the Elder and the Legend of St. Christopher in Early Flemish Painting," *Art Quarterly*, XIII, 1950, p. 38.

[69] Patinir may have had in mind the motif of the frightened bather on the distant shore in the painting of St. Christopher by Bosch, now in Rotterdam (illus. in Baldass, *H. Bosch*, 1960, pl. 78).

[70] *Loc.cit.*

41

with Charon's Boat" (Fig. 54). It is also today in the Prado, having been providentially saved from a fire in the Palace of Madrid in 1734. It is an appropriate work to place at the end of the Master's career, even though it may have pre-dated some of the others of the late period, because of its eschatological nature; namely, Patinir contrasts the Christian Earthly Paradise with Hell, in a single composition that is not dissimilar to a triptych by Bosch. Hell becomes at the same time the classical Hades, and the composition features the ferryman Charon, directing his flat-bottomed boat toward it across the choppy waters of the Styx (or Acheron). His lone, nude male passenger seems already to have noticed the cavernous portal of Hades and its guard, the triple-headed dog Cerberus (Fig. 55). Replacing the traditional mediaeval monster-mouth, Hell's entrance becomes architectural and is appropriately ornamented with a chain of toads, a motif invented by Bosch for the hell wing of his *Last Judgment Altarpiece* (Vienna, Academy).[71] Hell itself is a comparatively tame and rational landscape, very different from the "total, unenvironed and compulsive creations of Bosch." Still, it was Bosch who created the sixteenth century image of the fires of Hell. He also divined an architecture for Heaven that was neither Gothic nor Romanesque, in the *Garden of Earthly Delights*; and Patinir, in turn, creates a globular, crystalline *Fons vitae* from which issue the four rivers of Paradise (Fig. 56). Animals of many kinds, including the unicorn, gather about a lake, while others seem to erupt from an enigmatic, Boschian, protoplasmic creation at the left margin of the composition. Only partly visible, the form contains a globe, within which a figure—the Creator?—may be detected. Nearer at hand, a peahen is courted by a peacock, traditional symbol of Paradise,[72] while near the river bank is the pair of rabbits and a doe. Two angels escort blessed souls beside neatly rounded, heavily fruited trees in the Garden of Eden, while in the far distant fields there are countless other angels and souls who have somehow managed to get into heaven without the sanction of a Last Judgment. In the immediate foreground is the "still life" of rocks-seashells-iris of the Christopher composition, now of course lacking the evil salamanders but including the beneficial coral. The idyllic garden continues across the river in the foreground, where there is a parrot with other birds, blossoming rose vines, and a white Madonna lily. There is also a monkey, agent of the Devil in the temptation of Anthony, suggesting that this area on the "wrong" side of the river might be a sort of Christian Limbo. Or it might simply have been conceived for a compositional rather than iconographic reason, allowing a measure of visual continuity between the two sides of the picture to avoid an overly static rigidity. The panorama is surveyed from a point of view more elevated than in any composition

[71] Illus. in Baldass, *H. Bosch*, 1960, pl. 49. On pp. 225-26 Baldass suggests that this triptych may have been the copy of a huge one, now lost, by Bosch.

[72] Patinir had earlier used the peacock as a symbol of the perfect justice and holiness of St. Jerome, in the Metropolitan Triptych (see above, p. 35).

since the early landscape with St. Catherine (Fig. 6), though in marked contrast to that picture the panel is given an almost diagrammatic clarity through the bilateral symmetry of parts. The river that usually meanders across a composition now describes a plane which moves straight back from foreground to the blinding light of the horizon, Patinir's most stunning evocation of the romance of infinite space.

Most remarkable perhaps is the fact that there is evidently no surviving precedent at all in Western art for a composition in which the central subject is Charon's boat, and its innovation must be credited either to Patinir himself or else to the patron who may have commissioned the painting.[73] The myth of Charon was, of course, well known in Northern Europe, mainly because of its appearance in the sixth book of the *Aeneid*. Virgil does not make Charon diabolical, as Dante does in the third canto of the *Inferno*, but rather presents him as the somewhat pathetic figure that we find in Patinir:

> . . . Charon is here,
> The guardian of these mingling waters, Charon,
> Uncouth and filthy, on whose chin the hair
> Is a tangled mat, whose eyes protrude, are burning,
> Whose dirty cloak is knotted at the shoulder.
> He poles a boat, tends to the sail, unaided
> Ferrying bodies in his rust-hued vessel.
> Old, but a god's senility is awful
> In its raw greenness.[74]

The angel that beckons on a nearby hillock, and the Earthly cathedral silhouetted against a blue hill on the far side of Eden,[75] may have given consolation to the later owner of the picture, Philip II. It would have provided a hope of salvation, we may imagine, hardly to be found by the King in the several Bosch paintings of Paradise in his possession.

WORKSHOP

Like all master painters of his day Patinir would have had assistants in his studio, and in fact Dürer's diary confirms this. Although the brief lists that com-

[73] There was at least one equivalent, no longer in existence, in the ancient world: Pausanias describes a masterpiece on this subject by Polygnotos, painted around 460 B.C. in the Hall of the Cnidians at Delphi (*Description of Greece*, ed. by A. R. Shiletto, II, London, 1886, Bk. x, Ch. XXVIII, pp. 271-73).

[74] *The Aeneid of Virgil*, tr. Rolfe Humphries, New York, 1951, p. 154. Among published edi-

tions in the early 16th century was the illustrated copy issued by Grüninger in Augsburg in 1505. Its Charon scene bears no resemblance to that of Patinir.

[75] The angel is reminiscent of the one in Bosch's *John on Patmos* (Berlin), and here too, on the horizon, is a cathedral city (illus. Baldass, *H. Bosch*, 1960, pl. 85).

prise the archives of the Antwerp painters' guild do not record that he enrolled any pupils officially, we may nonetheless assume that assistants were responsible for some of the replicas, reduced copies, and variant compositions of works by the Master. These paintings were either produced on order, as was probably the case in the pictures purchased by Lucas Rem, or else for stock to be sold from the studio or at fairs. There are in addition a number of original compositions in the style of Patinir that do not seem to be autographic but which may have been produced in his workshop. And finally there are other paintings more or less in his style that appear to be later creations. These paintings, often good but sometimes poor, are attributed to Patinir primarily for want of another name. Among his followers with styles that are definable are Cornelis Massys, Lucas Gassel, Herri met de Bles, and the Master of the Half-Lengths. Because of the still current confusion with the work of Patinir of some of the paintings by the Master of the Half-Lengths I have thought it well to define his landscape style in a separate chapter, and to include a separate catalogue of his landscape paintings (Cat. IV).

The difference between "original," "replica," and even workshop product was not nearly so keenly felt in the sixteenth century as it was to be later. There was little outright faking in the modern sense, except in the realm of the fine-art print, as Dürer discovered to his distress; so that when one master adopted a composition from another, as did Joos van Cleve when he appropriated Patinir's landscape setting for his *Rest on the Flight* (Brussels), we may reasonably assume that the originating master, who was proud of his accomplishment, may well have felt complimented. And of course there were occasional collaborative enterprises between master painters, such as the Patinir-Massys *Temptation of St. Anthony*—a symptom of the new era in Antwerp painting of subject-matter specialists which was to reach its apogee a century later in the workshop of Rubens.

Relatively few paintings of the Early Netherlandish school bear signatures, though many probably were signed originally on frames that were later replaced. Bosch, Massys, Gossart, and Van Orley occasionally signed, whereas Gerard David and Joos van Cleve apparently never did. Patinir erratically affixed his signature not only to one of his finest but also to one of his weakest works (Figs. 8, 1). A modern interpretation of the absence of signatures would be that the masters of those days, unlike our own, were not compelled by the need to authenticate their work; and thus a major preoccupation of the art historian today has been the problem of attribution.

In my catalogue of the paintings of Patinir I have included under the originals the replicas, copies of smaller size, and variant compositions. Usually no attempt has been made to separate the hand of the Master himself from that of a studio

assistant, though the paintings in question vary greatly in quality. Five original compositions by Patinir are known to me which exist either as replicas of approximately the same size, or as more or less faithful copies smaller in size. As listed and briefly discussed in the catalogue under the prototype these are: *Burning of Sodom* (Rotterdam), two copies; *Martyrdom of St. Catherine* (Vienna), one copy; *Preaching of John the Baptist* (Brussels), two copies; *St. Jerome* (Louvre), one copy; *St. Jerome* (lost original; a second variant original in London), two copies. With the exception of the painting of St. Jerome now in the Louvre, all of the aforementioned originals are relatively small pictures and hence could be duplicated with relative ease. As far as I know copies were not made, or have not survived, of the four large, late works. It seems likely if not inevitable that of the pictures that were copied, one was made while the painting was still in Patinir's studio; though one must not rule out the possibility that a copy could have been made later by an artist totally unconnected with the studio. Drawings may have been made, if not of entire compositions at least of portions that were particularly appealing. Evidence for this may reside in the fact that the *Triptych with Rest on the Flight* (Kaufmann-Kaus Collections), a commissioned altarpiece, would not have remained in the studio; yet the main composition of both figures and landscape was rather closely adapted in a picture painted for Lucas Rem a number of years later. Apparently studio drawings were either destroyed or else consumed in the process of transmittal of design, for there exists today, as far as I know, not a single drawing contemporary with Patinir which copies any of his painted compositions, in whole or in part.

Of special interest in this connection is the heretofore undescribed *Triptych with St. Jerome* in a private collection in Palermo (Fig. 36). It is a rather ambitious work that resembles the Metropolitan Museum *Triptych* in its approximate size, curved upper frame, and subject matter. It is different however in a number of ways. The featured figures of St. John the Baptist (baptizing and preaching, on the left wing), St. Jerome (extracting the thorn from the lion's paw, in the center), and St. Anthony (reading, on the right wing) are in very small scale and bear no relationship to the figures of the New York painting. They have been poorly rendered by a hand other than that of the Master himself. Since the landscape is also of mediocre quality and has been derived from two additional compositions by Patinir, as discussed earlier in this chapter (p. 34), we are on relatively safe grounds in considering the triptych in its entirety as a workshop production.

The most popular themes in Patinir's repertory were Jerome in the Wilderness, of which he made five different original compositions, and the Rest on the Flight, of which there are at least four from his hand. I have found no replicas of any of Patinir's compositions of the Rest on the Flight, though the landscape vistas that he

45

created for them proved to be of great appeal and were copied and adapted in many variant compositions by other painters.[76] I have discovered and incorporated in the catalogue nine such pictures. Several of these nine paintings combine motifs from two of the original compositions by Patinir. These are: the *Rest on the Flight* in the Collection of Mrs. Kidston in Bristol (Fig. 19), one in the National Gallery in London (Fig. 57), one in Brussels, No. 350 (Fig. 58), one in the Comte de Vogüé Collection in Dijon (Fig. 59), and one in the Johnson Collection in Philadelphia (Fig. 60).[77] Since these are pastiches, like the Palermo Triptych, that involved knowledge of more than a single painting by Patinir, logic would suggest that all were produced in the studio, as a result of the demands made upon it. One hesitates however to reach this conclusion since they are so disparate in style that each appears to have been painted by a different hand. They also vary in quality, with the painting in Dijon being much the best. It is safest to leave open the question of whether pictures such as these might have come from the workshop, or could have been produced by anonymous painters not connected with it.

From the large number of other works that were painted under the influence of the style of Patinir I have chosen several for brief discussion. The first is a *St. Christopher* (Switzerland, Private Collection?) (Fig. 53), which without question depends on Patinir's picture in the Escorial (Fig. 49). The quality of the painting appears to be high, and the huge crystalline world-sphere behind the Child is a clever idea that I have discussed above. The scale relationships and somewhat loose technique do not seem to be those of Patinir himself. While the painting might have been produced in his studio, I feel that it is better viewed as the somewhat later production of a follower.

A thinly veiled reinterpretation of the Louvre *Landscape with St. Jerome* (Fig. 26) exists in a small variant composition of which at least three examples have survived (Figs. 63-65). The kneeling figure of the penitent Saint seems to have been adapted from Patinir's Metropolitan Museum *Triptych* (Fig. 35). Perhaps the orig-

---

[76] Four vistas were of special appeal and were adopted as follows: 1. The Miraculous Wheatfield with village and distant landscape, originating presumably in the Kaufmann-Kaus Triptych (Fig. 16); copied or adapted in paintings in Minneapolis (Fig. 21), Bristol (Fig. 19), and Doorn (cat. no. 8c). 2. Port City on a river, with bridge, stylistically strongest in a picture in Dijon (Fig. 59), and possibly originating in a lost composition by Patinir; copied in paintings in London (Fig. 57), and Brussels, no. 350 (Fig. 58). 3. Pagan Temple complex, originating in the Prado *Rest* (Fig. 39); incorporated in the London composition in addi-

tion to the Port City motif; added to the Bristol composition along with the Miraculous Wheatfield. 4. Distant Vista with Grazing Ass, chateau and horseback rider, originating in the Lugano composition (Fig. 12). This not particularly distinguished landscape was oddly enough the most popular in the repertory of Patinir. It was adopted at least twice by Joos van Cleve, and it recurs in the following paintings from the Patinir shop or by a follower: Rotterdam (fragment?) (Fig. 13), Philadelphia (Johnson Coll.) (Fig. 60), and Stockholm (Fig. 62).

[77] Cat. Nos. 20, 21, 23, 25, and 32.

inal of these variants is the one formerly in the hands of the New York dealer Frederick Mont (Fig. 63), for here the story-telling details are in greater abundance and are more meaningful. The one owned by Wildenstein and Company (Fig. 65) is particularly fine in color, and despite abrasions it presents a crisp appearance. One or all of these panels might have originated in the Patinir workshop. I find no reason to believe that they are copies of a lost original by Patinir himself.

More distant from the autograph style of the Master is a picture with the familiar theme of the *Baptism and Preaching of John*, recently in the hands of a dealer in Switzerland (Fig. 67). That the figures of Christ and the Baptist bear a direct relationship to those on the left wing of the Palermo Triptych (Fig. 36) might qualify this painting (as its forged signature in the left-hand corner does not) as a product of the studio, though it may well be later in date.

More disturbing is the problem presented by a large painting of high quality and great beauty, the *Rest on the Flight* in the Collection of Mrs. Dorothy Hart, which I saw when it was exhibited in Bruges in 1956 (Fig. 61). Alien to the style of Patinir, I believe, are all of the figures, the branching of the trees in the woods at the left, and the plants in the foreground; but in many other respects, such as the treatment of the earth and the far distant landscape, the painting is extremely close to the Master himself.

There are a number of paintings, in addition to those by the Master of the Half-Lengths, which represent the continuation of Patinir's landscape style after his life-time. Two of these, both quite small, are the *Flight into Egypt* in the National Gallery in Washington (Fig. 68), and the *Temptation of Christ* in the Bearsted Collection, Banbury (Fig. 66). The construction of the distant landscape is weak in both pictures; and the former has long been recognized as the work of a Flemish "follower" as late as ca. 1550, primarily on the basis of its figure style. A third painting that might be placed in the category of a later follower is the *Flight into Egypt* in the Museo Arte Catluña in Barcelona (Fig. 71). It bears a vague resemblance to Patinir's early picture of the same subject in Antwerp (Fig. 4), especially to the figure group of the Holy Family in the lower right corner; but the sleeping shepherd(?) in the central foreground, and the general atmospheric quality speak the language of a style of painting practiced by the generation that followed Patinir's.

Also by a later follower, I believe (and notwithstanding the fact that it is "signed"), is the intriguing *Landscape with Shepherds* in the Michel de Pret-Roose Collection (Fig. 69). With its enigmatic subject and altogether unorthodox, subtly unbalanced composition, this recently discovered painting is a curious combination of naïve and sophisticated elements. There are reflections here of Patinir's youthful style, as seen in the Karlsruhe *Jerome* (Fig. 1—compare the silhouetted plants and shaded ground rills, and the profile of the distant mountain); but there is also a rather hard,

linear clarity in the organization of the elements of the receding landscape that points to the stylistic accomplishment of a painter akin to the Master of the Half-Lengths, working probably in the 1530's.

In addition to the aforementioned pictures there is a fairly large group in public and private collections that I have neither discussed nor attempted even to list—paintings that reflect the style of Patinir in an ever diminishing degree.

CHAPTER THREE

FIGURE STYLE AND PROBLEMS OF
COLLABORATION

IT HAS long been recognized that Patinir engaged noted Antwerp painters to paint the large-scale figures in at least two of his larger and more important landscape paintings. His action heralded a new era which saw the rise of the specialist artist, and it constitutes one of the earliest known instances in Northern European painting of collaboration between independent master painters who ran their own workshops. The two pictures are the *Temptation of St. Anthony* (Fig. 44), and the *Rest on the Flight* in Berlin (Fig. 40). It is a quasi-documented fact that Quentin Massys painted the figures in the former;[1] the figures of the Virgin and Child in the latter are unquestionably in the style of Joos van Cleve, painted by himself or a member of his atelier.[2] The problem of the figure style, or rather styles, that appear in other indisputable paintings by Patinir that contain large figures has scarcely been discussed in the literature, for it is a thorny one indeed.

It was probably around 1521-22, late in what one can surely assume was a prematurely terminated career, that Patinir turned to the dean of figure painters in Antwerp; and Quentin Massys produced for him the subtly balanced figure group that commands the foreground of the *Temptation of St. Anthony* (Fig. 45). Even lacking documentation, one would have little difficulty recognizing the hand of Massys here, not only in the distinctive individual figure style but also in the well-unified psychological interplay that brings the group together. The same style pervades the large figures in two other masterworks produced by Patinir at about the same time, the Madonna and Child in the Prado *Rest on the Flight* (Fig. 41), and St. Christopher with the Christ Child in the Escorial picture (Fig. 50). The Madonna sits in majestic isolation, in full control of a landscape in which she must compete, so to speak, with a proliferation of natural beauty and human activity in the background. With the rather bulky, statuesque quality of a nursing Madonna by Robert Campin, the figure displays quite clearly the archaizing style of Massys. Her lumi-

---

[1] This is attested in the 1574 inventory of the collection of Philip II in the Escorial: the figures are "de mano de maestre Coyntin" and the landscape "de maestre Joaquin" (*Museo del Prado, Catalogo de los Cuadros*, Madrid, 1952, p. 469). Carl Justi made the discovery ("Altflandrische Bilder in Spanien und Portugal, Joachim Patinier und Quentin Metsys," *Z.f.b.K.*, XXI, 1886,

pp. 93-94).

[2] Baldass, 1918, p. 119, sees the hand not of the Master himself but of a follower. The pose of the Madonna warming her hand by a fire was ultimately derived from a composition by Robert Campin (Master of Flémalle) (Baldass, *loc.cit.*); and it is also adopted by other artists in Antwerp contemporary with Patinir.

nous, bluish-white mantle; the fur-lined robe, the edge turned back to reveal a brocaded sleeve; and the contrast of broad drapery folds with very fussily rumpled ones about the Child, all point to this. The head of the dark-haired Child is characteristic of Massys, as well as the face of Mary, with her long nose, small, firm chin, and dark, downcast eyes. The same artist undoubtedly painted the figures of St. Christopher, the Christ Child, and the aged hermit nearby (Figs. 49-51). The ruddy-fleshed, hirsute and dark-bearded Christopher, with a very prominent nose, is from the repertory of Massys, even though the pose of the figure, awkwardly bent forward to suggest effectively the supernatural weight upon his back, may have been inspired in its design by Albrecht Dürer, either through his engraving of the Saint dated 1521 (B 51) or else one of the figure studies of Christopher now lost that Dürer prepared for Patinir in Antwerp in the same year.[3] It is difficult to decide whether Patinir himself, Quentin Massys with the help of an assistant, or Massys alone painted these figures. If Patinir did paint them it would represent a remarkable and highly successful effort on his part to assimilate so thoroughly the style of another painter, though this is by no means an impossibility.

The large figures that appear in two earlier paintings by Patinir are in a very different style and have nothing to do with Massys. These are the *Baptism of Christ* (Fig. 8) and a related work, the *Triptych with Rest on the Flight* (Figs. 16-18), both painted, I believe, shortly after 1515 when Patinir became freemaster in the Antwerp guild. As long as a century ago the English scholar Weale noted that the figures of Christ and John the Baptist in the former painting were an adaptation of those created by Gerard David in Bruges for the central panel of his great triptych of the Baptism; and Weale even went so far as to suggest that David enlisted the services of Patinir to paint the landscape.[4] However close the harmony between the figures in the paintings by Patinir and by David, Patinir has not attempted to copy David, and there are considerable differences in style. There is a distinctive type of John the Baptist in the Patinir painting, a figure whose face has rather pinched features and whose forehead is covered with heavy forelocks. The same person reappears on the left wing of the *Triptych with Rest on the Flight*; and it was surely painted by the same hand. If this figure reminds us of David's Baptist, the Madonna of the central panel does not reflect David's type at all. Her plump face, rounded forehead, and slight chin are among the features of a figure style that no one has been able to pinpoint, except in one or two other paintings that M. J. Friedländer once felt were painted by Patinir.[5] That Patinir would have enlisted the assistance of some other

[3] E. Panofsky, "Noch Einmal 'Kopie oder Fälschung?,'" *Z.f.b.K.*, LXII, 1928-29, p. 182; J. Held, *Dürers Wirkung auf die Niederländische Kunst seiner Zeit*, The Hague, 1931, p. 67.

[4] *Le Beffroi*, III, 1866-70, p. 342. M. Conway

concurred with Weale (1921, p. 351).

[5] The Madonna is somewhat related to a half-length *Madonna* (formerly London, Heseltine Coll.) that Friedländer ascribed to Patinir (IX, 1931, no. 227, taf. XCIII). I feel that the Heseltine

figure painter, as yet unidentified, for these two pictures seems unlikely, though it is certainly not impossible. I am inclined to agree with Hulin de Loo, who long ago insisted that Patinir himself painted not only the beautiful landscape of the central panel of the triptych but also the staffage.[6] Again, as is the case of the monumental figures in the style of Quentin Massys in the late works of Patinir, the question arises whether our landscape specialist was sufficiently versatile to have produced these large-scale figures, especially in view of the fact that they appear so suddenly in the development of his landscape pictures.

Patinir did paint figures; and he furthermore created a figure style that is quite consistent in all but the earliest of the paintings that I have attributed to him. This style is relatively accomplished in the medium-sized figures in the foreground of the Metropolitan Museum *Triptych* (Fig. 35), and more so in the large grisaille figures on the exterior wings (Fig. 38). It may also be clearly observed if we examine photographic details of the small figure group in the background of the Vienna *Baptism* (Fig. 9), and of the disciples of Christ in the foreground of the Johnson Collection *Assumption of the Virgin* (Fig. 25). Characteristic of this style are the faces, which often have dark and staring eyes, long and sharply defined noses, and large ears. Beards are frequently long and carefully combed. More telling is the treatment of the hands, which are generally large and clumsy, and wrists that are very thick or, by preference, not visible at all. The bare foot is usually curved on its outer edge from heel to little toe, and the big toe is given an unusual emphasis—most prominent in the figure of Charon (Fig. 55). Robes are ample but rather closely fitting, defining smooth surfaces and falling to the ground in simple masses. The drapery is now and then bunched in fine folds, as in sleeves, and it is sometimes defined in impasto highlights.

The draughtsmanship of the little figures in the two earliest known works, the Karlsruhe *Jerome* (Fig. 1) and the Antwerp *Flight into Egypt* (Fig. 4) is cursory to say the least, but it may be rationalized if we assume that the creative energy of the young artist was absorbed in his new venture of designing a landscape in which figures were of secondary interest. His facility in figure painting would seem to have improved as he matured and paid more attention to this element of the compo-

---

Madonna figure, as well as the slight and primitive landscape against which she is posed, bears little or no relationship to the certain works of Patinir. It was apparently copied from a fine painting by Bernart van Orley, a picture recently in the Hallsborough Gallery, London, and now in an English private collection (illus. in I. Bergström, *Den Symboliska Nejlikan*, Malmö, 1958, fig. 15).

A second painting composed of figures and very little landscape that Friedländer ascribes to Patinir is a *Crucifixion* now in the Portland, Oregon, Art Museum (IX, no. 224, taf. XCII, when in Madrid, Schlayer Coll.). An attribution to Patinir is at best highly dubious.

[6] Bruges Exhibition of 1902, *Catalogue critique*, p. 54.

sition. Not surprisingly Patinir turned to Bosch for inspiration, and the influence is very apparent in the swarm of malefactors—soldiers in colorful costume and armed with a variety of weapons—who flee from their momentarily unsuccessful attempt to murder St. Catherine (Fig. 6). Picturesque Boschian rustic types with expressive faces are also found in the group to which the Baptist preaches in the background of the painting in Vienna (Fig. 9). One member of this group, the prominent man with pointed nose and wearing a turban, seems unquestionably to have been derived from Bosch's *Mocking of Christ*, in the Escorial. Later Patinir succeeds in evoking the forms of Bosch, without copying directly, whenever he needs to represent ugliness or the works of Satan, as in the background of the *Temptation of Anthony* (Figs. 44-46).

At the heart of the problem of the interrelation of the style of Patinir's middle period with the styles of master painters who were contemporary with him in Antwerp lies the question of his relationship with Joos van Cleve. That the two masters collaborated was stated by Karel van Mander, whose imagination and ear for hearsay were somewhat keener than his factual knowledge and eye for style. He reported seeing in the collection of Melchior Wijntgis three paintings by Patinir and one by Joos van Cleve of a "very beautiful Madonna" to which Patinir had added an "especially pretty landscape."[7] Patinir's painting of the *Rest on the Flight* now in Berlin (Fig. 40) could be this very picture. Another (unlikely) candidate, suggested by Friedländer, is a painting attributed to Joos van Cleve that is now in the Louvre and depicts the *Virgin and Child with Dominican* (Fig. 70);[8] or else a workshop variant picture (Fig. 72) which combines this landscape with the Madonna from the Master's painting of the *Rest on the Flight* now in Brussels (Fig. 14).[9] The iconography of the landscape that appears in these two pictures is so close to that of Patinir that one could think of collaboration if the execution were not so weak. A fourth possibility of an existing painting that might have led Van Mander into thinking it a work of collaboration is the Brussels picture itself (Fig. 14).[10] This fine little painting confused such a good modern critic as Carl Justi, who believed that Patinir painted the landscape behind a Madonna unquestionably in the style of Joos van Cleve.[11] The confusion is not without good reason, for Van Cleve has copied, with very few changes, the landscape setting of Patinir's *Rest on the Flight* that is today

[7] For Van Mander's account see above, Chapter I, p. 8, n. 28.

[8] *Landscape, Portraiture, Still Life*, New York, n.d., p. 47. E. Michel, *Le Louvre, Catalogue Raisonné, Peintures flamandes du XVe et du XVIe siècle*, Paris, 1953, pp. 72-73 (no. 2018B; 0.57 x 0.55).

[9] The variant picture was formerly in Schleissheim, now in Munich, Alte Pinakothek, no.

839. Friedländer lists the picture (IX, no. 49a) as a replica, with different landscape, of the Brussels *Rest* (see the following note).

[10] Friedländer IX, no. 49. *Musées royaux des Beaux-Arts de Belgique, Cat. de la Peinture Ancienne*, 1949, p. 31 (no. 349; 0.54 x 0.675; acquired in Paris in 1884 as a work by Patinir).

[11] Mentioned by Friedländer, IX, p. 119.

in the Thyssen Collection in Lugano (Fig. 12).[12] Van Cleve likes the two landscape vistas on either side of the Patinir composition so well that he reuses them later in a different context, as the background for an *Enthroned Madonna with Angels* (Liverpool, Weld-Blundell Collection).[13] In reciprocation, so to speak, and as a further attestation of the closeness of collaboration between these two Masters and their workshops in Antwerp, the girlish Madonna of the Van Cleve Brussels *Rest* reappears with but slight changes in a variation of the theme which was produced in the Patinir studio, a painting now in the London National Gallery (Fig. 57).[14] The style of the landscape in Van Cleve's painting in Brussels (Fig. 14) is distinctively though subtly different from the style of the Patinir painting which it emulates (Lugano). The brushwork of Joos is more fluid and more assured than that of Patinir. Though he paints with precision, like the landscape Master, he tends to worry less about detail. The earth, here seen in his typical warm, brownish-tinged patches of soil, is organized in a somewhat more rhythmical and in a sense more restless manner than that of Patinir. Typical in the landscapes of Van Cleve—and strongly accentuated in this composition—is the twisted rock formation behind the Madonna, with vistas of earth and sky seen through irregular openings. His treatment of rocks tends to be more like that of Quentin Massys, usually softer and more rounded in light and shade. Patinir's rocks tend to be both rougher and at the same time more carefully ordered in irregular layers that he carefully keeps parallel to the picture plane.

Patinir's landscape formula seems to have exerted a decisive influence early in the problematic career of Joos van Cleve, whose style of landscape painting was never to undergo fundamental change. This led Friedländer to remark that in no painting of Joos can landscape be found that differs essentially from that of Patinir.[15]

Since the early career of both Masters is cloaked in uncertainty, it is well to review briefly the theories of modern scholars on the matter. Joos van Cleve enrolled as freemaster in the Antwerp guild in 1511, Patinir in 1515. Ludwig Baldass, who wrote in 1925 the only monograph that has appeared on Joos van Cleve, believed that the artist worked in Bruges prior to 1511, since he feels that the strongest influence on his early style is to be found in the paintings of Hans Memling, with those of Gerard David also an important influence.[16] Since David's Bruges Triptych of the Baptism of Christ influenced Patinir's treatment of the same subject (Vienna), circumstantial evidence could point to the possibility that Joos and Joachim were to-

[12] The Brussels painting is catalogued and described by L. Baldass, *Joos van Cleve*, Vienna, 1925, no. 7, p. 16 of catalogue.

[13] *Ibid.,* no. 34, abb. 36, dating ca. 1520; Friedländer, ix, no. 67, dating ca. 1525. Best reproduction in Friedländer, *From van Eyck*

to Bruegel, N.Y. (Phaidon Press), 1956, pl. 200.

[14] Van Cleve's own studio also repeats the Madonna (see n. 9 above).

[15] ix, p. 120.

[16] *Op.cit.*, pp. 6ff.

gether in Bruges prior to 1511. Baldass believes that the Brussels *Rest* by Joos van Cleve must be dated before 1515, for stylistic reasons, and his guess is ca. 1510, the same date to which he would assign the Louvre *Virgin and Child with Dominican* (Fig. 70), which also shows the influence of Patinir.[17] I feel strongly that Patinir's Lugano *Rest*, from which Van Cleve copied the landscape for his own *Rest* (Brussels), cannot possibly be dated as early in the career of Patinir as 1510. If the landscape of the *Virgin and Child with Dominican* had been copied after a lost original by Patinir, as Baldass suggests, the putative model would also have to be dated after 1510. This rather weak landscape appears to me to have been composed of iconographical elements from the later repertory of Patinir (notably the Prado *Rest*, compare with Fig. 43, detail).

Friedländer has cleverly adduced proof that Joos van Cleve's earliest training was in Kalcar on the Lower Rhine, in the workshop of Jan Joest; and he is inclined to agree with Baldass that Van Cleve might have gone to Bruges after 1508, when the Kalcar workshop was dissolved.[18] No date is assigned by Friedländer to the Brussels *Rest*, though he is generally inclined to advance by two to five years the dates Baldass surmises for the works of Joos van Cleve. Pending a more precise clarification of the early style of Joos van Cleve, and the separation of his oeuvre from the works by assistants and followers, I see no reason to date either the Brussels *Rest* or the Louvre *Virgin and Child with Dominican* before 1515-16, a date which would logically explain their relationship to the works of Patinir in Antwerp. I would also like to repeat my admittedly unproved theory that Patinir may have been in Antwerp before 1515, when he enrolled as freemaster. In Antwerp he could not only have seen a number of works by Bosch, important for his early style, but he could also have enjoyed the company, after 1511, of Joos van Cleve.[19]

Even Quentin Massys and his workshop succumbed to the appealing breadth and clarity of the Patinir world landscape formula, notwithstanding the fact that

---

[17] *Ibid.*, no. 6, p. 16 of catalogue.

[18] IX, pp. 58-62.

[19] Pure fantasy is the hypothesis of G. J. Hoogewerff that Joos van Cleve worked in Genoa during the years 1512-15, and further, that Patinir worked there with him (*Het Landschap van Bosch tot Rubens*, Antwerp, 1954, p. 22). The same author stated earlier that Patinir, in Genoa, painted the landscape in Van Cleve's *Crucifixion Triptych* in Naples ("Joachim Patinir en Italie," *Revue d'art*, XLV, 1928, pp. 124ff.); and Hoogewerff maintains this view in *Vlaamsche Kunst en Italiaansche Renaissance*, Malines-Amsterdam, n.d. (ca. 1947), p. 104. This triptych, painted entirely by Joos, and surely

in Antwerp (ca. 1512 according to Baldass, *op.cit.*, no. 19, abb. 16; and ca. 1516 according to Friedländer, IX, no. 11, p. 128), is remarkably close in landscape style and in motifs to the Van Cleve Brussels *Rest*, as well as the Louvre *Madonna with a Dominican*. I feel that the Naples Triptych was painted at the same time and hence agree with Friedländer's dating.

Of other paintings attributed to Joos van Cleve with landscape backgrounds that are close to the style of Patinir, I should mention the *St. Anne with the Virgin and Child* in Modena. Baldass dates it ca. 1512 (*op.cit.*, no. 17, abb. 13), while Friedländer again prefers a dating of ca. 1516 (IX, no. 45).

Massys was an excellent painter of landscape in his own right, as may be witnessed in the two magnificent landscape backgrounds of the *Altarpiece of St. Anne* (Brussels), dated 1509, and in the landscape of the *Rest on the Flight* today in the Worcester Museum, of about the same date.[20] He found the Patinir formula suitable notably for a group of three paintings, two of which are triptychs, depicting the *Crucifixion*.[21] They have been dated around 1520, during the period of known collaboration between Massys and Patinir. Though Friedländer was inclined to believe that the landscapes in these pictures could have been painted by Patinir, Baldass gives a fine stylistic analysis to demonstrate that they are in the style of Massys and not Patinir, however much the influence.[22] In another late painting by Quentin, a Leonardo-inspired *Virgin and Child with St. Anne* (Poznań, Poland, National Museum), the landscape is so close to the style of Patinir that Friedländer also believed that it must have been the work of Patinir.[23] Here however, as in the paintings of the Crucifixion, it appears to be the Patinir formula in its most mature phase, applied not by himself but by a follower.[24]

Art historians and connoisseurs have claimed to see the hand of Patinir in the backgrounds of many Flemish paintings of the sixteenth century, in addition to the ones discussed above. My study of the problem has convinced me that in not one single picture is this the case. Owing to the fact that Patinir's idealized and formula-bound landscape was not only attractive but rather easily assimilated, it was imitated by many artists, including Joos van Cleve, Quentin Massys, and Adriaen Isenbrandt. Its assimilation by the Master of the Half-Lengths was so complete that it will be discussed separately in the next chapter.

[20] Friedländer, VII, nos. 2 and 4a, pls. II, III, XI.

[21] The triptychs are in the National Gallery, London, and in the Mayer van den Bergh Museum, Antwerp (M. Davies, Nat. Gal. Cats., *Early Netherlandish School*, 2d ed., 1955, pp. 69-70, with detailed bibliography; Joz. de Coo, Mus. Mayer van den Bergh, *Catalogus I*, 1960, pp. 99-101. The single panel, formerly in the Prince of Liechtenstein Gallery, was acquired in 1954 by the National Gallery of Canada, Ottawa (R. H. Hubbard, *European Paintings in Canadian Collections*, Toronto, 1956, p. 58, Pl. XXIX). All were products of Massys' studio, with the degree of participation of the Master himself open to question.

[22] Friedländer, VII, pp. 52-53; Baldass, "Gotik und Renaissance im Werke des Q. Metsys," Vienna *Jahrbuch*, NF, VII, 1933, pp. 155-56.

[23] VII, p. 47 and taf. XXI; and IX, pp. 118-19.

[24] Friedländer's opinion was rejected by G. Glück and by Baldass, who cautiously gives the landscape to a follower of the late style of Patinir (*op.cit.*, pp. 157-58, 171). That it may have been painted by Quentin's son Cornelis is suggested by C. van de Wetering, *Die Entwicklung der niederländischen Landschaftsmalerei vom Anfang des XVI bis zur Jahrhundertmitte*, Berlin, 1938, p. 56; and by J. Białostocki, *Europäische Malerei in Polnischen Sammlungen*, Warsaw, 1957, no. 128, pp. 497-98, color pl. VI (detail).

CHAPTER FOUR

THE MASTER OF THE HALF-LENGTHS

THE unidentified painter of the early sixteenth century who suffers under the appellation "Master of the (Female) Half-Lengths" specialized not only in the painting of figures, as his name suggests, but also in landscapes.[1] He is the only artist who continues the landscape style of Patinir in such a deceptively close manner that misattributions continue to be made, for his style has never been given adequate definition. He should be given credit for a number of paintings, some of very fine quality, that pass today as works by Patinir.[2] More important, reattribution of these works to him will enable us to bring the style of Patinir into sharper focus.

M. J. Friedländer compiled a list of sixty-seven paintings, plus replicas, in his catalogue of the works of the Master of the Half-Lengths.[3] Nearly fifty percent of these depict a doll-like, well-dressed figure of a young lady, often with a finely wrought ointment jar (in possible allusion to the Magdalene), who either reads, writes, or plays a flute or spinet.[4] The Master of the Half-Lengths and his workshop also conducted a profitable business in religious triptychs, which in his time were enjoying what has been called an assembly-line manufacture for export, and also in stereotype compositions of the Madonna and Child against a dark background. He further produced a few mythological subjects, newly fashionable in Northern Europe

---

[1] In French the name is *Maître des Demi-Figures* (*de Femmes*), and in German it is *Meister der weiblichen Halbfiguren*, the name with which he was baptized in the 19th century. He was first signaled as a personality by Waagen in 1866. Bibliography cited in note 8 below.

[2] For example, certain attributions by F. Winkler in *Thieme-Becker*, 37, 1950, p. 351; G. J. Hoogewerff, *Het Landscap van Bosch tot Bruegel*, Antwerp, 1954, p. 25; A. Bengtsson, "A Painting by Joachim Patinir," *Idea and Form*, Stockholm, 1959, pp. 88-94.

[3] *Altniederländische Malerei*, XII, 1935, nos. 46-113 (71 and 75 are identical). Another painting is added in vol. XIV, 1937, *Nachtrag*, p. 127. He illustrates only three paintings: *Knee-Length Madonna and Child* with landscape background (Paris, Trade, taf. x), *Half-Length Magdalene Reading* (Munich, Trade, taf. XI), and *Judgment of Paris* (The Hague, Mauritshuis, on loan from the Rijksmuseum, taf. XII).

[4] S. Bergmans has recently observed that the presence of the jar does not necessarily imply that the lady is intended to be the Magdalene but simply indicates social status (*Le siècle de Bruegel* [Cat. Exh. Brussels Museum], 1963, p. 171).

The two main sizes of the paintings are about 20 x 16, and 10 x 8 inches. The phenomenal popularity of this image is affirmed by its repetition in Bruges in the workshop of Isenbrandt (Friedländer, XI, nos. 211-13) and especially in the shop of Ambrosius Benson (*ibid.*, nos. 274-75, with a dozen repetitions). G. Marlier recently expanded the Benson list by ten pictures, all of the lady reading and/or holding a jar (*Ambrosius Benson*, Damme, 1957, nos. 93-109, 192-94, and 231-35). Thus around 30 known copies and variations of this pseudo-religious theme were made in Antwerp and Bruges—a large number of which were surely exported.

for sophisticated tastes, and more than a dozen surviving pictures which are essentially landscape paintings with religious themes, in the fashion of Patinir. Friedländer's catalogue lists five paintings in which landscape plays a dominant role, all but one depicting the theme of the *Rest on the Flight*.[5] I have added to this group half a dozen paintings which I believe were incorrectly ascribed by Friedländer to Patinir,[6] and as many more that this scholar did not list. None of the paintings attempts the ambitious size of Patinir's masterworks, being mostly between one and two feet in height and about two feet in width. Even though the list is incomplete, (see Catalogue IV) it may serve a useful purpose,[7] and I have reproduced all the paintings in it.

Several scholars have tried to produce convincing evidence for a positive identification of the Master but none has yet succeeded.[8] Over half a century ago Wickhoff tried to identify him with Jean Clouet, French court painter and father of the famous François; Wurzbach suggested Lucas de Heere, painter and poet of Ghent. More recently Otto Benesch developed a proposal that the Master was a Bruges painter named Hans Vereycke, of whom Van Mander wrote briefly, praising him as both portrait and landscape painter.[9] The basis for Benesch's identification is unhappily most insecure, resting mainly upon the appearance of the name "Hans Vereycke," written in a sixteenth century hand, on the blank reverse of a landscape drawing in the Louvre. The style of this drawing, and of many others that Benesch proposes to give to Vereycke, is by no means certainly that of the mysterious Hans Vereycke, with whom Benesch identifies the Master of the Half-Lengths.[10] Other reasons for rejecting this proposed identity are easy to muster. First, although the Van Mander

[5] XII, nos. 70, 71 (75), 76, 77, 80. No. 79 may be another.

[6] IX, nos. 222-223, 243b, 244, 256, 257(?).

[7] Paintings in which the landscape plays a subordinate role are discussed in this chapter but not included in the catalogue; nor do I include paintings known to me which seem relatively remote from his autographic style.

[8] For earlier bibliography on the Master see: C. van de Wetering, *Die Entwicklung der niederländischen Landschaftsmalerei* . . . , Berlin, 1938, p. 37; and Winkler, *loc.cit.* The problem of the identity of the Master has been recently discussed by E. Michel, *Cat. raisonné des peintures flamandes du XVe et du XVIe siècle au Musée du Louvre*, Paris, 1953, pp. 160-61; by G. Marlier, *op.cit.*, pp. 58-59, and 191, n. 24; and by S. Bergmans, *op.cit.*, p. 170.

A beginning attempt to sort the hands at work on the female figures has been made by Marek Rostworowski, who suggests that Marcellus Coffermans might be one of the artists ("Netherlandish Paintings in Polish Collections," *Burlington Mag.*, 102, 1960, pp. 366-68; this is a review of an exhibition "Netherlandish Paintings, 1450-1550, from Polish Collections," National Museum of Poland, Warsaw, May-June 1960, cat. by Jan Białostocki).

[9] Benesch's article bears the promising title "The Name of the Master of the Half-Lengths," *G.d.B.-A.*, LXXXV, 1943, pp. 269-82. He includes Van Mander's account of Vereycke on pp. 272-73. Before Benesch, Baldass had suggested that the Master of the Half-Lengths was Vereycke ("Drei Jahrhunderte flämische Malerei," *Pantheon*, V, 1930, p. 133, n. 1; noted by Marlier, *op.cit.*, p. 191, n. 24).

[10] In any event I fail to see a relationship between these drawings and the style of landscape painting of the Master of the Half-Lengths.

"Vereycke" does not appear in the Bruges archives, a painter named Jan van Eeckele may be the same person, as Hulin de Loo proposed long ago.[11] Van Eeckele became freemaster in the Bruges painters' guild in 1534, dying there about 1561. "Vereycke" would seem to have been primarily a painter of landscape, and even one who—to cite Van Mander's ambiguous remark—"worked from nature"; whereas the Master of the Half-Lengths was primarily a figure-painter and one whose well-ordered landscapes, as much as his pretty ladies, are lacking in invention and might truly be called "hot-house flowers."[12] Further, the Master of the Half-Lengths must have spent most of his career working not in Bruges but in Antwerp, and possibly also Malines, as his strong dependence upon the landscape style of Patinir and upon the figure style of Bernard van Orley suggests.[13] If he were in fact Hans Vereycke (alias Jan van Eeckele), it is most improbable that he would have left Antwerp for Bruges in 1534, thus going against the strong artistic current which flowed in just the opposite direction.[14] But the most important reason for not accepting the identity, in my opinion, is that the landscape style of the Master of the Half-Lengths, so very close to that of Patinir, could hardly have started as late as 1534, in or outside of Antwerp, and have continued until past the mid-century, which must have been the case with the paintings of Vereycke-Eeckele. By the middle of the fourth decade of the sixteenth century, ten years after the demise of Patinir, the mode of landscape painting was being transformed into a more naturalistic one in the hands of specialists like Cornelis Massys and Herri met de Bles; and it was surely no later than this, during the third and fourth decades of the century, that the Master of the Half-Lengths was continuing the manner of Patinir, by then old-fashioned.[15]

I can profitably begin my discussion of the Master of the Half-Lengths with two indisputable and characteristic works which represent his mature figure style, as well as the style of his landscape, and his particular landscape "iconography." These are very similar compositions which represent the Holy Family as it rests on the flight, one in the London National Gallery (Fig. 73),[16] and the other in the

---

[11] *Catalogue critique*, Bruges Exh. of 1902, pp. xxx-xxxiv.

[12] I cannot agree with Marlier's suggestion that Hans Vereycke might have painted the landscape backgrounds which appear in pictures with figures by the Master of the Half-Lengths (*op.cit.*, p. 59, n. 21). Baldass was the first to propose, correctly I feel, that the Master painted his own compositions in their entirety, landscapes as well as figures ("Die niederländische Landschaftsmalerei von Patinir bis Bruegel," Vienna *Jahrbuch*, 34, 1918, pp. 126-27).

[13] Friedländer, XII, 1935, p. 27, is an advocate of Antwerp. S. Bergmans suggests Malines

[*op.cit.*, p. 170].

[14] Friedländer, *loc.cit.*, suggests that he was one of the many artists who had worked in Bruges but moved to Antwerp when Bruges's fortunes waned.

[15] The styles of costume worn by his elegant ladies and the small figures of hunters in his landscapes, while admittedly an uncertain criterion for dating, seem to be no earlier than this period (Baldass, *loc.cit.*).

[16] It measures 0.81 x 0.62. M. Davies, Cat. National Gallery, *Early Netherlandish School*, rev. ed., 1955, p. 89, no. 720; *Plates*, London, 1947, 79.

Johnson Collection in Philadelphia (Fig. 74).[17] The Holy Family group is composed of stereotypes that are readily recognizable when they recur in reduced size in his landscape paintings proper. Mother, Father, and Child all wear sweetly idealized but somewhat vacuous expressions. The Madonna is as perfectly self-composed as one by Raphael, and she is trimly though not ostentatiously attired. Her hair is carefully coiffed with a center part and braids that are covered by a gauze headpiece. The chubby and completely nude Child reaches for fruit offered by a venerable and fatherly Joseph with balding head, and long, forked, gray beard.[18] Flesh parts are softly modeled, cool and enamel-like, rather bloodless and boneless for all of their perfection. One detail of Mary's costume in the Philadelphia composition appears almost as a signature in almost all of the other Madonna figures that the Master paints: a small, round, metallic button which fastens the bodice, or occasionally is placed at the waist.[19]

In these two compositions the foreground stage, so to speak, is enframed by a tree with a mossy trunk. It is more or less in correct scale with the figures, so that only the leaves of its lowest branches are visible. Beyond the grazing ass in both landscape backdrops one finds segments of Patinir-like landscape arranged in a neat and orderly manner. Using his mentor's ideas as to what an ideal nature should be, and appropriating a large number of his motifs, the Master of the Half-Lengths produces a very stable landscape. Although he employs the general color scheme of Patinir, the glazes are much thinner, and he tends to soften and give greater variety to the greens of the middle distance, and to mix the far-distant blues with green or grayish

[17] It measures 0.825 x 0.58. W. R. Valentiner, *Cat. of the Johnson Collection*, II, no. 389, reprod. It was in the Bruges Exh. of 1902, No. 264, illus. M. J. Friedländer, *Meisterwerke . . .* 1903, taf. 78, and p. 29: "well the prettiest devotional picture from the hand of the Master." Discussed and illus. as a work by "Hans Vereycke" by Benesch, *op.cit.*, p. 270, fig. 3.

Among other similar paintings of the Madonna and Child in a landscape, I should like to mention two. The first is in the Coll. Comte d'Ursel, Bruges (0.82 x 0.575); it was also in the Bruges Exh. of 1902, no. 266, illus. in Friedländer, *Meisterwerke . . .*, taf. 79, and included in his catalogue of the Master's work in XII, no. 70. The background depicts the small figures of the Holy Family, during the Flight, upon a broad, tree-lined road leading directly back into the landscape. This rather startling forecast of Hobbema's *Avenue at Middelharnis* (London, Nat. Gal.) caused C. van de Wetering to feel that it must have been painted by an anonymous master who was more advanced in his landscape style than the Master of the Half-Lengths (*op.cit.*, pp. 38-39, abb. XXXIVb). De Wetering also reproduces and discusses a half-length Madonna in a landscape that was formerly in the Coll. Baroness Ferstel, Vienna (*loc.cit.*, abb. XXXIVa; Friedländer, XII, no. 66). I believe that both of these landscapes are by the Master of the Half-Lengths.

[18] The preferred fruit for the Christ Child in many of his compositions is a brown-skinned pear, a replacement for the symbolic apple usually held by or offered to the Child in earlier Flemish painting.

[19] Noted by Friedländer, XII, p. 30. To confuse matters, it may also be found in a painting of the *Madonna and Child* in a landscape in the Wadsworth Atheneum, Hartford, Conn., attributed to the School of Adriaen Isenbrandt. Both landscape and figure style are very close to the Master of the Half-Lengths. Acc. no. 1957.606.

green for better tonal unity. Clouds are frequently swept across the sky in stratified layers, so that he gives the effect of stability even in this changeable and evanescent aspect of nature. Though lacking in these two compositions, flights of birds are usually seen, a decoration avoided by Patinir but frequent in Antwerp landscape painting in the 1530's and 1540's.[20]

In his paintings of landscapes proper, there occurs a characteristic treatment of the foreground terrain that is different from that of Patinir. The ground is frequently carpeted with blades of grass and nondescript small plants which are sharply delineated in impasto brush strokes as they sparkle in light against a dark green ground. Such foregrounds are seen to good advantage in the *Flight into Egypt* in the North Carolina Museum of Art in Raleigh (Fig. 81), and in the *Rest on the Flight* in Vienna (Fig. 79). He likes to include one distinctive little plant that occurs in abundance in the Vienna composition and is not found in the works of Patinir: a small variety of fern with a slender, ladder-like frond, painted with single brush strokes. On foreground paths he often scatters pebbles of various sizes, a detail enjoyed by Adriaen Isenbrandt and others but not by Patinir. His types of trees are somewhat varied; foreground trees bear larger leaves and their trunks and upper branches are much more in evidence than is usual in the works of Patinir, who prefers the Bosch-type of formalized, neatly rounded tree with straight trunk. As in a Patinir the foreground trees are often delicately vine-clad; but new is the greater attention paid to the bark of the trunk. Delineated by light, vertical strokes, the tree appears to be a member of the oak family. The Master of the Half-Lengths likes to include the apocryphal palm-tree which bent down to offer its fruit at the command of the Child, a motif found in both the Raleigh and Vienna pictures but never in the several interpretations by Patinir of the Holy Family's flight into Egypt. He adopts from Patinir's compositions the spindling tree whose branches and sparse foliage are silhouetted against the sky, as seen to good advantage in the Copenhagen *Rest* (Fig. 87), and a *Landscape with Hunting Party* that was formerly in the Wesendonk Collection in Berlin (Fig. 85).

In his desire for a landscape even more thoroughly tamed by man than Patinir's, the Master of the Half-Lengths frequently includes a massive castle, studded with tiny windows, chimneys, crenelations, and square and rounded towers. It usually crowns and completely fills the top of a rocky rise of ground, as we have seen in the London and Philadelphia pictures of the Holy Family at rest on the flight. Similar castles may be found in the painting in Raleigh, and in the Uppsala *Landscape with Scenes of John the Baptist* (Fig. 83). Like the occasional small castles and the multitudinous farmhouses of Patinir, which exist in endless variation in design, so the architecture of the anonymous Master is never exactly repeated in copybook

[20] Noted by Baldass, 1918, p. 127.

fashion, as might be expected from a painter who rejoiced in quantity production.[21]

"Manneken pis" fountains are prominent in the foregrounds of the London and Vienna compositions of the *Rest on the Flight* (Figs. 73, 79), the one in the latter with an architectural base containing Italianate ornament. The statuettes are like winged cupids, and by their action they reveal the increasingly lighthearted approach of artists to religious themes as the sixteenth century develops. With greater decorum it is the son of Venus who recurs in an appropriate setting in a little painting of the *Judgment of Paris* (The Hague), which has been attributed to the Master;[22] and Cupid is also an ironically fitting accouterment in his *Landscape with the Death of Lucretia*(?) (Brussels, Trade) (Fig. 90). In Patinir's compositions of the Rest on the Flight, one frequently finds in the distance, as a tiny figure, the "Egyptian idol" which toppled at the very nearness of the Christ Child. The Master of the Half-Lengths does not miss the chance to bring the idol to the foreground (Vienna [Fig. 80]; Basel [Fig. 91], and New York Historical Society [Fig. 89]), where he is able to display his participation in the pseudo-classical spirit of Antwerp by means of elaborate colonettes.

Other staffage elements taken from Patinir include the farmer with the two-horse team, and the participants in the scene of the miraculous wheatfield. For the latter, however, he creates a personal iconography which is used with complete consistency. The wheat that has been cut is gathered in neatly spaced sheaves, ready to be bound; while the soldiers of Herod as a troop, a banner waving in the breeze, confront the master of the wheatfield. This is most easily observed in the near distance of the Vienna *Rest* (Fig. 80), and it occurs in the far distance of all of the other paintings of the subject. The group is even included as a tiny scene in the far distance of the Raleigh *Flight into Egypt*, a magnified study of which (Fig. 82) reveals a freedom of brush strokes never enjoyed by Patinir. The consistent use of such details as these constitutes a fixed vocabulary that points to the origin of the paintings in a single workshop, though all were not necessarily painted by the Master himself.

The broad landscape design of the Master of the Half-Lengths usually includes, like Patinir's, a distant port city and bay. The mature phase of his style represents a clear-cut advance over that of Patinir in the disposition of elements on a flatter ground, which extends with a greater illusion of aerial perspective depth to the horizon line.

[21] City walls and castles are a notable pre-occupation of the artists who made the drawings of the famous Herrera Sketchbook (Brussels, Museum), surely an Antwerp product and made during the lifetime of the Master of the Half-Lengths. Sometimes (wrongly, I feel) attributed to Patinir, the sketchbook may well be mainly the work of Cornelis Massys (the recent opinion of E. de Callataÿ, "Cornelis Massys paysagiste, collaborateur de son père et de son frère et auteur de l'album Errera," *Bulletin des Musées Royaux des B.-A. de Belgique*, 14, 1965, pp. 49ff.).

[22] Friedländer, XII, taf. XII.

Though the landscape components tend to remain as in Patinir parallel to the picture plane, the transitions are more deft and the scale relationship of parts is better. As Baldass observed, the perspective achievement of the Master comes from the latest works of Patinir; but his technique, with precision in the rendering of details, comes from the somewhat more linear style of Patinir's middle period.[23] This may be clearly seen if the "Wesendonk" *Landscape with Hunting Party* (Fig. 85) is compared with Patinir's *Landscape with St. Jerome* in the Prado (Fig. 28). In the concept of Patinir, how much greater is the feeling of "world landscape," in breadth, in variety of landscape phenomena, and in the illusion of remoteness from the viewer—in short, in romantic appeal. The same clear difference in outlook may also be felt in the anonymous Master's *Landscape with Scenes of John the Baptist* (Uppsala; Fig. 83), a painting which has always been attributed to Patinir. Here a panoramic landscape of extraordinary extent is rather more realistic, in the photographic sense, than any work by Patinir; but to the modern eye at least it lacks the excitement, the tensions, and the spatial contradictions of the style of painting which it seeks to emulate.

I believe that it is possible to define an early landscape style for the Master of the Half-Lengths. It would seem to appear in two paintings which have also until now been attributed to Patinir. The first is a *Landscape with St. Jerome* in Zurich (Fig. 75), which I have proposed is a copy by the Master after a lost painting by Patinir. The putative lost original, discussed earlier, also exists in a mediocre workshop copy today in Elberfeld; and its left portion is an independent copy of sufficiently fine quality to warrant attribution to Patinir himself (London; Fig. 30).[24] In the Zurich copy by the Master of the Half-Lengths, not only does the figure style of St. Jerome, who is inappropriately dressed for the occasion in his red cardinal's robes (Fig. 76), appear to be uncharacteristic of Patinir, but the entire landscape becomes alive with human activity quite to the taste of the anonymous Master. Unrelated to the story of Jerome, for example, is the pair of turbaned figures prominently placed in the left foreground, one pointing to the landscape. He also fills the composition with animals and birds, including an owl and magpie—birds that are repeated in another comparatively early picture, the Vienna *Rest* (Fig. 79). Here too the peacefully nibbling rabbits of Patinir come to life and leap about in excitement. The rock masses of the Zurich *Jerome* have been greatly softened, quite unlike those of Patinir, and they are dotted with vegetation. Also already as a hallmark of his own early style, as it differs from that of Patinir, one finds sparkling blades of grass and other plants, including the thin-leaved fern, carpeting the foreground. Patinir's peaceful landscape has been activated.

All of these characteristics may be seen in another early work, the splendid

[23] *Loc.cit.*

[24] See above, p. 33.

variation on the theme of Jerome in the wilderness that is now in the Nelson Gallery in Kansas City (Fig. 77, and 78, detail). The Saint loses his centered position as the Master gives almost equal attention to the merchant caravan, which he expands to six camels as against the two which invariably appear in Patinir's many paintings of the theme. He borrows from his Zurich composition the detail of men chopping wood (presumably the monastery monks), but he changes the incident of the sleeping lion and theft of the monastery ass by the merchants to tell the tale, on the road in the foreground, of the later recovery of the ass. Exuberantly he adds other incidents of rural life unrelated to the story but of interest for their own sake, such as a scene outside a tavern, and the activities of a forge. One architectural detail, stemming perhaps from Patinir's single use of it in the Berlin *Rest* (Fig. 40), becomes a virtual signature: a low-arched bridge near the foreground, parallel to the picture plane. There are many flights of birds; and in the far distance is a steep rock formation, inclined at an angle, and with a mesa-like hill before it, which he will repeat with regularity in almost every later composition.

The next painting in the Master's landscape development might have been the Vienna *Rest* (Fig. 79), which remains like the Kansas City *Jerome* a somewhat restless and very detailed composition. His characteristic figure style is now on the verge of maturity. From the beginning he tended to activate the little figures that dot his landscapes by having them raise an arm to point or gesture, as do the soldiers in the wheatfield here, and also the pair of turbaned strollers in the Zurich *Jerome* (Fig. 75), one holding a pike while the other points into the landscape. They reappear in the Uppsala *Landscape with Scenes of John the Baptist* (Fig. 83) and are featured in another fine painting now identifiable as a work by the Master in the Randall Collection in Montreal, a *Landscape with the Preaching of the Baptist* (Fig. 86).

His fully developed style of both figure and landscape painting is unmistakable in such a picture as the beautifully preserved *Flight into Egypt* in Raleigh (Fig. 81), a work heretofore regarded by Hoogewerff and others as a collaboration between Patinir and the Master of the Half-Lengths. The additional works listed in my catalogue also appear to be the mature products of the Master himself or of his workshop; and there are no doubt others with which I am not acquainted.

The Master of the Half-Lengths not only must have conducted a large workshop but must have worked in collaboration with other painters, though not with Patinir. Of the landscape paintings in the catalogue only one has a figure style that is clearly not his own. This is a *Rest on the Flight* in the New York Historical Society (Fig. 89). These figures may have been added by another anonymous artist in Antwerp, the so-called Master of 1518, identified with a large group of loosely related paintings that were assembled by Friedländer for which an autograph style has yet

to be clearly defined.[25] Further, there is the problem of a large and beautiful painting in the Art Gallery of Toronto which features the Madonna and Child in the theme of the Rest on the Flight. Here the style and iconography of the landscape is completely that of the Master of the Half-Lengths, while the figure style is that of Bernard van Orley.[26] Both Orley's Madonna and the Half-Length Master's landscape represent the developed styles of the two artists, and this suggests a date no earlier than the late 1520's. It seems clear that the Master of the Half-Lengths had derived his own style of the sweet and aristocratic female figure from Orley's style of around 1521-22, seen in such paintings as the *Job Altar* in Brussels and the *Holy Family* in the Prado, which are signed and dated in these two years.[27] This female type reflects the courtly style that Bernard van Orley developed in Brussels and Malines around 1518 when he was appointed painter to Margaret of Austria. It was adopted by the Master of the Half-Lengths, and he was apparently quite content to remain with this lovely stereotype throughout his career, just as he was perfectly satisfied with a landscape style that he had derived from Patinir.

Among other problems that remain to be resolved in landscape paintings of the Patinir milieu, an interrelated one is that of the style of Adriaen Isenbrandt.[28] Though he was evidently a pupil and close follower of Gerard David in Bruges, paintings have been attributed to him which reveal so thorough a knowledge of the works of Patinir that even today they are sometimes given to him.[29] There are other paintings

[25] XI, 1934, pp. 44ff. and nos. 70-103. Cf. the motif of angels helping Joseph gather fruit in the background of the *Madonna with Saints* (Rome, Stroganoff Coll.) attributed to the Master of 1518, no. 79, taf. XXXIX.

Georges Marlier has recently proposed that the Master of 1518 is one Jan van Dornicke, one of whose daughters married Pieter Coeck van Aelst ("Des révélations sur Pieter Coeck d'Alost," *Connaissance des Arts*, no. 164, Oct. 1965, p. 113); expanded in the same author's *Pierre Coeck d'Alost*, Brussels, 1966, pp. 112ff.

[26] It measures 0.86 x 0.73; P. Brieger, "Van Orley's 'Rest on the Flight into Egypt,'" *Art in America*, XXVI, 1938, pp. 182-84, reproduced.

[27] M. J. Friedländer, VIII, 1934, no. 85, taf. LXVII, LXIX, and no. 140, taf. XCI; on the influence of Raphael on the latter picture see p. 111. Van Orley's influence on the Master of the Half-Lengths is noted in XII, p. 29.

[28] On Isenbrandt see especially E. von Bodenhausen, *Gerard David und seine Schule*, 1905, pp. 207ff.; Friedländer, XI, pp. 79ff.; M. Davies, *op.cit.*, pp. 131-32.

[29] There are two especially fine landscape paintings by Isenbrandt that depend on a first-hand knowledge of Patinir's works. The first is a *Rest on the Flight* (Vienna), which shows the dual influence of David and of Patinir's Thyssen Coll. *Rest* (Baldass, 1918, pp. 122-23, fig. 7; Friedländer, IX, p. 122, remarks: "very close to Patinir in the landscape, and I once thought of collaboration."). The second landscape is a *Flight into Egypt* (Berkshire Museum, Pittsfield, Mass.); Baldass, 1918, pp. 124-25, figs. 8 & 9; Friedländer, XI, no. 150: "landscape in the manner of Patinir," changing his earlier opinion that Isenbrandt and Patinir collaborated on the picture (*Von Eyck bis Bruegel*, 1916, p. 184, when in the Thiem Coll., San Remo). Hoogewerff continued to believe in collaboration, and evidently was unaware of Baldass' important article, since he wrongly declared that he reproduced the picture for the first time; he also made the erroneous remark that the picture is dated 1515 ("Joachim Patinir en Italie," *Revue d'art*, 45, 1928, p. 117, fig. 1). It had been reproduced earlier by K. Gerstenberg, *Ideale Landschaftsmalerei*, Halle, 1923, pl. IV, 1, as his only illustration of a painting by "Patinir."

which seem to reveal an influence of the landscape style of Jan Wellens de Cock,[30] while still others are related in both figure and landscape style to the Master of the Half-Lengths.[31] One example by Isenbrandt, a *Landscape with St. Hubert* (Berlin-Dahlem) (Fig. 92) will illustrate the proximity of his eclectic landscape style to that of the Master of the Half-Lengths.[32] The difference is most clearly perceptible in Isenbrandt's distant landscape of rolling fields, curved walls and towers, and a city of many small buildings defined in sparkling highlights. Depending on one's point of view, the landscape styles of both of these painters may be deemed to be but a step away from that of Patinir.

A hypothetical reconstruction of the early career of the Master of the Half-Lengths is now possible. He was probably trained in the early 1520's, and it is tempting to think that this took place in the studio of Joachim Patinir. There he might have painted the Zurich *St. Jerome* (Fig. 75), copying a now lost Patinir original, and there he would have absorbed the Patinir iconography from a number of other paintings. He soon developed a consistent style of landscape painting that differed from that of his Master, however closely it remained bound to it. At the same time, in the early 1520's, the anonymous Master would seem to have developed a figure style based upon that of Van Orley, a painter with whom he may have later collaborated. Until these hypotheses can be resolved and the Master identified, he at least can be recognized as not only a painter of pretty ladies but also a landscape painter of some importance in Antwerp in the second quarter of the sixteenth century, however retardatory his style in the Patinir manner.

Vaguely related to the Pittsfield painting and more in the Isenbrandt than Patinir milieu is the rather weakly constructed *Landscape with the Flight into Egypt* in the D. G. Van Beuningen Collection (D. Hannema, *Catalogue . . .*, Rotterdam, 1949, no. 27, pl. 32, as "Patinir"; Museum Boymans-van Beuningen, Rotterdam, *Catalogus Schilderijen tot 1800*, 1962, no. 2473).

[30] E.g. *The Magdalene in a Landscape*, London, Nat. Gal. (M. Davies, *op.cit.*, p. 132, no.

2585; reprod. *Plates*, 1947, 120); compare with a painting attributed to Jan de Cock by Friedländer in XI, pl. LI.

[31] See note 19 above, and Davies, *op.cit.*, p. 131.

[32] It measures 0.40 x 0.30. Königliche Museen zu Berlin, *Beschreibendes Verzeichniss der Gemälde*, Berlin 1883, no. 620, p. 335: "earlier called Herri de Bles; but it is more in the manner of Patinir"; 9th ed., Berlin 1931, p. 354, "School of Patinir."

CHAPTER FIVE

CONCLUSION

JOACHIM PATINIR apparently never created a landscape painting without an identifiable religious subject that was planned from the beginning and determined the mode of the setting. This was only partly the result of a continuing demand for a pictorial adventure with the cachet of a sanctified theme. Patinir himself, in all probability, would have considered a panel painting whose sole subject was nature—a pure landscape—without a true reason for being, a stage set without actors and hence without meaning. There had indeed been recent precedence in Netherlandish panel painting for the concept of nature without man, namely the exterior wings of triptychs by both Gerard David and Hieronymus Bosch; but these were parts subordinate to a larger whole and were isolated examples which proved to be without particular consequence either in the work of these two artists or in the development of the autonomous landscape.[1]

Drawings of pure landscapes were also made by Flemish painters at the time of Patinir and in the following decades. A few that have survived from the pre-Bruegel period appear to have been made directly from nature, but for the most part they are imaginary studio creations. They were made usually as preparatory sketches or ideas for paintings, or as studio exercises in landscape elements that were sometimes collected in sketchbook form.[2] No one has succeeded in identifying with certainty Patinir's own style of landscape drawing, though among the several possibilities that have been attributed to him there may well lurk one or two originals.[3] None of

[1] The panels by David, on loan from the Rijksmuseum to the Mauritshuis, The Hague, have been dated shortly after 1509 (K. G. Boon, *Gerard David*, Amsterdam, n.d., p. 51, n. 1, illus. pp. 54-55). The panels of Bosch, representing "The Creation of the World," are the outer wings of the *Garden of Delights Triptych* (Prado), and have been variously dated ca. 1500 and ca. 1510 (L. Baldass, *H. Bosch*, New York, 1960, p. 229, pls. 60-61).

It is interesting to recall that at this very same time in Italy Lorenzo Lotto includes a "pure" landscape as part of an altarpiece, the predella of the Asolo Altar, 1508 (see E. Gombrich, "Renaissance Artistic Theory and the Development of Landscape Painting," *G.d.B.-A.*, XLI, 1953, p. 338).

[2] On the famous Herrera Sketchbook (Brussels) see Chapter IV, n. 21. On a similar sketchbook in Berlin, and the question of drawings for and after a painting by Herri met de Bles see: R. A. Koch, "A Rediscovered Painting, 'The Road to Calvary,' by Herri met de Bles," *Record of the Art Museum, Princeton University*, 1955, 2, pp. 31-51.

[3] Five drawings, all but two quite different in style, have been attributed to Patinir: *Landscape with St. Christopher* in Berlin (Bock-Rosenberg, *Die Zeichnungen der Niederländischen Meister*, Berlin, 1930, cat. no. 6698); *Landscape with the Story of St. Christopher* in the Louvre (L. Baldass, "Joachim Patiniers Christophorus-Zeichnung," *Mitt. der Gesell. für vervielfältigende Kunst* [Beilage der *Graphischen Künste*], 51, 1928, pp. 23-24); *Rocky Landscape* in the Boymans-Van Beuningen Museum, Rotter-

these is directly related to any known composition that he painted; and until such a drawing turns up, or until a signature can be proved authentic, the problem will remain unsolved.

Patinir was not the first to present a "world landscape" as the setting for the theme of a painting. Although his older contemporaries Gerard David and Quentin Massys had moved in this direction in a number of compositions, it was Hieronymus Bosch who had really exploited the broad landscape setting and had made a real issue of unending space. Nevertheless, what these masters had done incidentally, Patinir elected to do professionally, and landscape became his major concern. Even when figures are given prominence in a Patinir composition, as in the Vienna *Baptism*, the landscape absorbs them and becomes the pictorial element which leaves the most lasting impression on the viewer. If we are to consider him as "the first landscape painter,"[4] it is because his specialization was decisive in establishing the autonomy of landscape painting as a subject *sui generis*.

Of the generation of landscape painters which followed Patinir in Antwerp, the Master of the Half-Lengths chose to continue the style, iconography, and subject matter of Patinir with very few changes. With certain modifications it was carried forward by Cornelis Massys, Lucas Gassel, and Herri met de Bles, all of whom created identifiable, individual styles. Though quite transformed through a preponderant emphasis on the doings of man, the landscape paintings of Pieter Bruegel continue to reveal their ultimate source of inspiration. Finally, though the influence of Patinir is scarcely to be felt in the new ideal of a decorative, classicized landscape as it is conceived by Gillis van Coninxloo, to say nothing of such Romanized expatriates as Matthew and Paul Bril, the style of Patinir continues to inform the approach of Lucas and Martin van Valckenborch, and other painters of the later sixteenth century who were the precursors in the North of the baroque landscape.

In the over-all development of Flemish painting, the achievement of Patinir should probably be considered to represent not so much a beginning as an end—the ultimate consequence of the development of the landscape background by the Flemish masters of the fifteenth and beginning of the sixteenth centuries. From this standpoint it is not hard to justify the oeuvre of Patinir as representing the last pos-

dam (Exhibition Cat., *De van Eyck à Rubens, Dessins des Maîtres Flamands*, Paris, Bibliothèque Nationale, 1949, no. 34, pp. 30-31, pl. x); and J. Białostocki, "Nouvelles Notes sur l'Album Errera," *Bull. des Musées Royaux des Beaux-Arts de Belgique*, 1955, 4, p. 234; and two *Studies of Forests*, one in the Albertina, Vienna, and the other now in the Coll. of L. V. Randall, Montreal (both were discovered and published by O. Benesch as "Patinir" in the *Annuaire des Musées Royaux des Beaux-Arts de Belgique*, I, 1938, pp. 34-37, abb. 2 and 3; Benesch later re-attributed them to "Hans Vereycke" in "The Name of the Master of the Half-Lengths," *G.d.B.-A.*, LXXXV, 1943, pp. 269ff., figs. 1 and 9).

[4] M. J. Friedländer, IX, p. 124.

sible stage in the development of the mediaeval world picture.[5] Lingering in the compositions of Patinir is the outlook of the mediaeval cartographer, when he surveys a vast panorama from a high eye level: each element of the landscape is represented more or less as it appears in reality, but the natural scale relationships are willfully and necessarily disregarded. Even in the late compositions of Patinir the viewer is routed through the picture from detail to detail and from scene to scene. Whereas the painter in Renaissance Italy insisted, as a rule, on keeping the spectator at a respectful distance from his composition by means of formal clarification and idealization, the painter in the Low Countries, as a rule, demanded close observation. He wished to involve the viewer as much as possible with details that were descriptive, that told a story if possible, that made an intellectual game of disguised symbolism when appropriate, and that expressed, quite simply, the virtuosity of the painter as a technician. To recreate the visible world in an illusional, three-dimensional microcosm, to create a splendid new unity of infinite parts, was the intent of Jan van Eyck, and it remained the aim of Joachim Patinir.

That landscape painting had its origin in Northern Europe in the Germanic countries, and not in Italy, is not by chance, for its way was not blocked by Renaissance anthropocentrism. Nor was the time accidental, for not until the early sixteenth century was man's faith in Christian dogma, and an orientation to salvation in a world beyond this one, sufficiently shaken to produce the climate of thought that enabled an Altdorfer and a Patinir to develop landscape as an independent branch of painting.

[5] This point of view is voiced by J. A. Raczyński, *Die Flämische Landschaft vor Rubens*, Frankfurt, 1937, p. 14.

CATALOGUE OF PAINTINGS

PART I of this Catalogue contains every picture that I believe was painted by Patinir himself, with or without collaboration or assistance. The paintings are numbered and arranged in a hypothetical chronological order. In this catalogue I have included replicas which are more or less exact, and copies that vary in detail and/or size, but which were probably made by Patinir himself or by studio assistants.

Part II, Workshop, includes a number of paintings which very probably were not produced under Patinir's supervision. They do, however, reveal so thorough a knowledge of compositional motifs in two or more original pictures by Patinir that I have thought it wise to assemble them under this category. Part III, anonymous Later Followers, comprises only five pictures. These serve to represent the continuation of the Master's style after his lifetime.

Many different hands—none as yet identifiable—produced the pictures listed in Parts II and III. I have found it expedient, and even necessary, to rely on the copying and adaptation of Patinir motifs as a basic criterion for bringing at least the semblance of a working order to a confusing mass of material. All of the pictures in the catalogue at one time or another have been attributed to Patinir himself. If a painting has not been included, the reader is to infer either that I do not know of it or that I have deliberately excluded the picture as not being sufficiently close to the style of Patinir to warrant consideration in this study.

Part IV lists paintings, essentially landscapes, which I believe were painted by the Master of the Half-Lengths or his workshop.

The paintings in Part I are arranged in what I feel to be a chronological order, whereas those in Parts II-IV follow M. J. Friedländer's system of classification according to subject matter.

I. PATINIR

1. LANDSCAPE WITH ST. JEROME (Fig. 1)
Karlsruhe, Kunsthalle (No. 144)
0.13 x 0.17   Signed, lower left corner: OPUS/JOACHIM · D ·/PATINIR
   Bibliography: Van Mander (Hymans ed.), I, Paris, 1884, p. 196. *Kat. der Gemälde-galerie . . . Karlsruhe*, 6th ed., 1910, no. 144, p. 57. M. J. Friedländer, 1916, p. 100. L. Baldass, 1918, p. 113. G. J. Hoogewerff, 1928, pp. 131-32 ("late work"). J. Lauts, *Kat. Alte Meister*, *Staatliche Kunsthalle*, Karlsruhe, 1966, p. 235.

2. LANDSCAPE WITH FLIGHT INTO EGYPT (Fig. 4; Fig. 5, detail)
Antwerp, Museum (No. 64, Ertborn Coll.)
0.17 x 0.21   Signed, lower left corner: OPUS/JOACHIM · D ·/PATINIR
   Bibliography: Signature deciphered and picture first published in 1835 (see S. Sulzberger, *La réhabilitation des primitifs flamands, 1802-1867*, Académie royale de Belgique, Classe des Beaux-Arts, *Mémoires*, XII, fasc. 3, Brussels, 1961, p. 151). A. Michiels, *Histoire de la peinture flamande,* IV, 2d ed., Paris, 1866, pp. 407-8 (criticizes picture). Van Mander (Hymans ed.), I, Paris, 1884, p. 196. Fierens-Gevaert, *Les primitifs flamands,* III, Brussels, 1910, p. 219, pl. CLXIII. M. J. Friedländer, 1916, p. 100. L. Baldass, 1918, p. 113. M. Conway, *Cat. of Loan Exh. of Flemish and Belgian Art*, Burlington House, London, 1927, no. 113, pl. LII. M. J. Friedländer, IX, 1931, no. 231, taf. XCIV. G. J. Hoogewerff, 1928, pp. 131-32, fig. 12. Antwerp Museum, *Beschrijvende Catalogus,* I, 1948, no. 64, p. 209. A. Lhote, *Treatise on Landscape Painting* (tr. W. J. Strachan), London, 1950, pp. 12-13, pl. II.

3. LANDSCAPE WITH BURNING OF SODOM (Fig. 2)
Rotterdam, Boymans-Van Beuningen Museum (No. 2312)
0.23 x 0.295
   History: P. de Boer, Amsterdam (trade); D. A. Hoogendijk, Amsterdam, 1925 (trade); Ch. A. de Burlet, Berlin, 1927 (trade); F. Koenigs Coll., Haarlem, on loan to the Boymans Museum 1935-40; currently on loan to the Museum by the Bruikleen Dienst voor's Rijksver-spreide Kunstvoorwerpen.
   Bibliography: L. Baldass, "Ein Landschaft von Matthys Cock," *Z.f.b.K.*, 61, 1927-28, p. 94, illus. (first publication, as an early work by Patinir). M. J. Friedländer, IX, 1931, no. 219; XIV, 1937, p. 119. Braam, *Art Treasures in the Benelux Countries, I, The Netherlands*, n.d., no. 4113. Boymans-van Beuningen Museum, Rotterdam, *Catalogus Schilderijen tot 1800*, 1962, no. 2312, p. 101. A. Marchal in *Le Siècle de Bruegel* (Cat. Exh. Brussels Museum), 1963, no. 188, illus. 48.
   Copy:
   a. Fig. 3. Oxford, Ashmolean Museum (no. 320)
      0.343 (roundel composition in square frame) A careful copy, simplified in detail. Formerly Cologne, Malmedé, 1935, sold 1936. *Bibliography*: M. J. Friedländer, XIV, 1937, p. 119. Ashmolean Museum Catalogue, 1951, no. 320. Exhibited *Scaldis*, Antwerp, 1950, no. 545.

71

NOTE: There is a crude, later, variant composition. It is also a roundel composition, in rectangular frame, 0.235 x 0.275. Present location unknown. Photo in Friedländer archive, R.K.D. The Hague, no. 24036. *History and bibliography*: Berlin trade, de Burlet, 1932; sold by Fischer, Lucerne, 29-30 Aug. 1933, cat. no. 224, taf. 33; exhibited Zurich, Kunsthaus, 1934, exh. cat. no. 110, pl. xxxix. Mentioned by M. J. Friedländer, xiv, 1937, p. 119, and in *Le siècle de Bruegel*, p. 145, under no. 188, as related to the problem of identification of the painting by Patinir presented to Dürer by the city of Antwerp.

Unrelated to the Rotterdam composition, not in the style of Patinir, and lacking the figures of Lot and his Daughters is a *Landscape with Burning Cities* now in the Bliss Collection, Dumbarton Oaks, Washington, D.C. This has wrongly been thought to be the painting presented to Dürer (*Jeroen Bosch, Noord-Nederlandsche Primitieven* [Cat. Exh. Boymans Museum, Rotterdam], 1936, no. 64, afb. 79).

4. LANDSCAPE WITH MARTYRDOM OF ST. CATHERINE (Fig. 6; Fig. 7, detail)
Vienna, Kunsthistorisches Museum (No. 1002)
0.268 x 0.44
Comments: Fig. 6 is from a photograph taken before 1954 when small strips were removed from the top and sides (old dimensions 0.28 x 0.49). The replica mentioned below, slightly larger in size, has been in and out of the London trade for many years. The Vienna version has somewhat more detail and sparkle, though both may be considered to have been painted by Patinir himself.

History: Archduke Leopold Wilhelm Coll., Brussels, no. 453 of Inventory of 1659, as "Civetto" (Inventory published in the Vienna *Jahrbuch*, I, 1883, p. cxi).

Bibliography: F. Willis, "Zur Kenntnis . . . ," *Monatshefte für Kunstwissenschaft*, VII, 1914, p. 45, abb. 4. M. J. Friedländer, 1916, p. 184. L. Baldass, 1918, pp. 114-15, fig. 3. M. Conway, 1921, pp. 352-53 ("Vienna version a school replica"). M. J. Friedländer, IX, 1931, no. 250, p. 159. Vienna, Kunsthistorisches Museum, *Katalog der Gemäldegalerie*, II, 1958, no. 278, taf. 48, p. 96.

Replica:
a. Present location unknown.

   0.385 x 0.485

   M. J. Friedländer, IX, 1931, no. 250a, then owned by London dealer Langton Douglas ("exact replica of equal quality"). M. Conway, *loc.cit.*, believes this the original. Color reprod. with detail in *Illus. London News*, 18 Apr. 1936, p. 675. Exhibited Colnaghi, London, Mar. 1938, no. 24, color reprod., lent by Bruce S. Ingram. Sold Sotheby, London, 11 Mar. 1964, no. 24, illus.

5. BAPTISM OF CHRIST (Fig. 8; Fig. 9, detail)
Vienna, Kunsthistorisches Museum (Inv. No. 981)
0.595 x 0.77   Signed near the bottom, center: OPUS/JOACHIM · D ·/PATINIER
Comment: Fig. 8 is from a photograph taken before 1954 when a small strip was removed from the top (old dimensions 0.68 x 0.77).
History: Archduke Leopold Wilhelm Coll., Brussels, no. 452 of Inventory of 1659, as "Patenier" (Inventory published in the Vienna *Jahrbuch*, I, 1883, p. cxxxviii).

Bibliography: Van Mander (Hymans ed.), I, Paris, 1884, p. 196. M. J. Friedländer, 1916, p. 100, p. 184. L. Baldass, 1918, p. 118. M. Conway, 1921, pp. 350-51. M. J. Friedländer, IX, 1931, pp. 105-6, no. 221, taf. XCI. Vienna, Kunsthistorisches Museum, *Katalog der Gemälde-galerie*, II, 1958, no. 279, p. 96.

6. LANDSCAPE WITH PREACHING OF JOHN THE BAPTIST (Fig. 10)

Brussels, Musée de l'Art Ancien (No. 1041)

0.353 x 0.452

Comments: The panel has been cut down slightly on both sides, and probably at the bottom. In all likelihood it was originally about the size of the Philadelphia replica, listed below, which bears the coat of arms of Lucas Rem.

History: R. Peltzer Coll. (Auction F. Muller, Amsterdam, 26 May 1914, p. 7, no. 12, reprod.). Munich, J. Böhler, 1915. Lent by F. Muller, Amsterdam, to Exhibit, *French and Flemish Primitives*, Toledo, Ohio, Museum of Art, 1935, no. 33. Acquired by the Brussels Museum in 1940 from Matthiesen, London.

Bibliography: P. Kuttler in *Der Cicerone*, 1913, pp. 414-16. M. J. Friedländer, 1916, p. 183. M. Conway, 1921, pp. 350-51. M. J. Friedländer, IX, 1931, no. 220a. Brussels, Musées Royaux des Beaux-Arts de Belgique, *Cat. de la peinture ancienne*, 1949, no. 1041, pl. XXVIII.

Replicas:

a. Fig. 11. Philadelphia, Museum of Art (acc. no. 44-9-2)

0.38 x 0.505

M. J. Friedländer, IX, 1931, no. 220, when in Coll. of R. L. Taylor, Philadelphia. This careful workshop copy lacks the tiny figures of John baptizing Christ by the river bank in the distance, present in the Brussels version. The Dove of the Holy Ghost however is present, so that either the copyist omitted the Baptism or the figures were lost in a later cleaning of the picture.

b. Present location unknown.

0.20 x 0.30

M. J. Friedländer, IX, 1931, no. 220b (saw it when in Munich, Trade, J. Böhler, 1917 and described it as "a rather exact replica" of the above pictures).

7. LANDSCAPE WITH REST ON THE FLIGHT (Fig. 12)

Lugano, Thyssen Coll. (No. 321)

0.315 x 0.575

Comments: The most influential of Patinir's compositions of the theme, it was copied in whole and in part a number of times, both within the workshop and apart from it. In addition to the copies mentioned below, see No. 25 (Fig. 60) and No. 26 (Fig. 62). There are photographs in the Friedländer archive (R.K.D., The Hague) of two other adaptations, seemingly mediocre: 1) Florence, private collection, the Madonna figure larger and different in design; 2) Coll. L. Moreno, Paris (0.55 x 0.72).

History: R. von Kaufmann Coll., Berlin (Sale Berlin, Dec. 1917, Part 2, no. 90). Eduard Simon Coll., Berlin (Sale Berlin, 1929, Part 1, p. 62, no. 23).

Bibliography: Hulin de Loo, Bruges Exhibition of 1902, *Catalogue Critique*, no. 200, p.

54. L. Baldass, 1918, p. 114, fig. 2. M. J. Friedländer, ix, 1931, no. 232 (and see comment on the landscape under his no. 49). G. J. Hoogewerff, 1954, pp. 25-26, fig. 14 ("possibly a pupil's work or perhaps by Joos van Cleve"). R. J. Heinemann, *Katalog Sammlung Schloss Rohoncz*, Lugano, 1958, no. 321, taf. 38.

Copy:

a. Fig. 13. LANDSCAPE WITH GRAZING ASS (Fragment?)

Rotterdam, Boymans-Van Beuningen Museum (no. 2474)

0.27 x 0.23 (overcleaned)

Comments: A close copy, with slight changes, of the left half of the above painting. It is probably the left portion of what may once have been a complete copy. It is possible that both reflect a lost original by Patinir (there are certain details here and in Van Cleve's copy [Fig. 14] lacking in the Lugano composition: the road by the meadow before the chateau, and the wing attached to the nearby watermill).

History: Coll. J. Cremer, Sale, Dortmund, 29 May 1929, no. 29. Goudstikker, Amsterdam, Dec. 1929. D. G. van Beuningen Coll., Rotterdam.

Bibliography: D. Hannema, *Cat. of the D. G. Van Beuningen Collection*, 1949, no. 28, pl. 31 ("possibly a fragment, originally twice as large"). Museum Boymans-Van Beuningen, Rotterdam, *Catalogus Schilderijen tot 1800*, 1962, no. 2474, p. 102.

Copy-Variant by Joos van Cleve:

Fig. 14; Fig. 15, detail. Brussels, Musée de l'Art Ancien (no. 349)

0.54 x 0.675

The distant landscapes on either side are derived from the painting now in Lugano, as first noted by L. Baldass, *Joos van Cleve*, 1925, no. 7, n. 32, pl. 11. M. J. Friedländer, ix, 1931, no. 49. (The picture is discussed in Chapter III.)

8. TRIPTYCH WITH REST ON THE FLIGHT (Fig. 18; Figs. 16-17, details)

Central Panel: Rest on the Flight into Egypt

Left Wing: St. John the Baptist (in the distance the Baptism of Christ and the Preaching of the Baptist)

Right Wing: Saint (Pope) Cornelius

Frankfurt a/M., Coll. Willy Kaus

H. 0.72 x W. 1.10; each wing 0.30 wide

Comments: Fig. 18 is made from a copy of the photograph now in the Friedländer photo archive in the R.K.D., The Hague. It was presumably made at the time of the Bruges Exhibition of 1902, shortly before the triptych was damaged by fire. Also in the above-mentioned archive are photographs showing the fire damage, and the first restoration thereafter.

History: R. von Kaufmann Coll., Berlin; damaged by fire in 1904 when in Kaufmann Coll.; not included in auction of the collection in 1917. Cologne, Malmedé, 1932. Strasbourg, Kramer Coll., 1940's. Munich, Interkunst, 1950's, from whom acquired by Mr. Kaus.

Bibliography: Hulin de Loo, *Catalogue critique*, Bruges Exhibition of 1902, no. 199, p. 54. M. J. Friedländer, 1916, pp. 109, 184, taf. 18. L. Baldass, 1918, p. 117. M. Conway, 1921, p. 350. F. Winkler, 1924, p. 216. M. J. Friedländer, ix, 1931, no. 218, pls. LXXXIX and XC, pp. 115-16 ("figures and landscape by the same hand"). E. Gérard, *Dinant et la Meuse dans l'histoire du paysage*, Lammersdorf, 1960, pp. 76, 103.

Variant Copies of the Central Panel:

a. Fig. 19. Bristol, England, Coll. Mrs. George Kidston. (See Cat. No. 20)

b. Fig. 21. Minneapolis, Institute of Arts. (See Cat. No. 24)

c. Doorn, Netherlands, Coll. A. Kleiweg de Zwann

   0.31 x 0.20 x 0.09 (curved at top)

   M. J. Friedländer, IX, 1931, no. 218a (saw it when in Amsterdam, Goudstikker, 1928: "middle panel a [very] free copy of the Kaufmann Triptych").

9. ASSUMPTION OF THE VIRGIN (Fig. 20; Figs. 22-25, details)

Philadelphia, Johnson Collection (No. 378)

0.57 x 0.55 (original frame)

   History: Coll. Friedrich Lippmann, Vienna. Coll. C. T. Yerkes, 1909.

   Bibliography: W. R. Valentiner, *Catalogue of the Johnson Collection*, II, 1913, pp. 37-38 (figures by another hand, that of an Antwerp Mannerist); and III, 1914, p. 214 ("coat of arms of Lucas Rem, probably painted about 1519"; translates Rem's motto as "If it goes well, it is given by God"). M. J. Friedländer, 1916, p. 184. L. Baldass, 1918, p. 114, n. 3. Conway, 1921, p. 351. M. J. Friedländer, IX, 1931, no. 226. Worcester-Philadelphia Exhibition of Flemish Paintings, 1939, no. 59.

10. LANDSCAPE WITH ST. JEROME (Fig. 26)

Paris, Louvre (No. 4126)

0.76 x 1.37

   History: Coll. J. K. Huysmans, Paris. Coll. Sir Joseph Duveen, who presented it to the Louvre in 1924.

   Bibliography: M. Conway, *Cat. of Loan Exhibition of Flemish and Belgian Art*, Burlington House, London, 1927, no. 120, pl. LV. M. J. Friedländer, IX, 1931, no. 245, taf. IC. G. J. Hoogewerff, 1954, p. 25 ("late work, ca. 1520-25"). E. Michel, *Louvre, Catalogue Raisonné . . . Peintures Flamandes du XVe et du XVIe Siècles*, 1953, pp. 236-38, fig. 140 ("*très usé*").

   Copy:

   a. Fig. 27. Venice, Ca d'Oro

      0.29 x 0.55

      A close copy, simplified in details, bearing the coat of arms of Lucas Rem. *Bibliography*: M. J. Friedländer, IX, 1931, no. 245a ("replica with slight changes"). E. Michel, *loc.cit.* ("can only be shop work; heavier and more maladroit"). G. J. Hoogewerff, 1954, p. 25 ("replica").

11. LANDSCAPE WITH ST. JEROME (Fig. 28; Fig. 29, detail)

Madrid, Prado (No. 1614)

0.74 x 0.91   Signed near the bottom, center: JOACHIM D PATINIER

   History: First mention in 1605 by Sigüenza when in the Escorial. Transferred to the Prado in 1839.

   Bibliography: José de Sigüenza, *Historia de la Orden de San Jerónimo*, 2d ed., II, Madrid, 1909, p. 557. Friedländer, 1916, p. 184. L. Baldass, 1918, p. 119 and n. 2. Conway, 1921, p. 354.

G. J. Hoogewerff, 1928, p. 130, fig. 9. M. J. Friedländer, IX, 1931, no. 240, taf. XCVII, pp. 111, 113, 158. A. Lhote, *A Treatise on Landscape Painting* (tr. W. J. Strachan), London, 1950, pp. 14-16, pl. 26. *Museo del Prado, Catalogo* . . . , 1952, p. 468, no. 1614. A. Marchal in *Le siècle de Bruegel* (Cat. Exh. Brussels Museum), 1963, no. 192, illus. 52.

12. LANDSCAPE WITH ST. JEROME (Fig. 30)

London, National Gallery (No. 4826)

0.365 x 0.34

Comment: Not a fragment, this is the left part of a variant composition of the Prado *Jerome* (No. 11, Fig. 28). The variant composition is copied in its entirety in the three paintings listed below.

History: Coll. R. Kann, Paris (cat. 1907, II, no. 107). Duveen Brothers. Coll. Mrs. Henry Oppenheimer; bequeathed to the National Gallery in 1936.

Bibliography: L. Baldass, 1918, p. 119, n. 2 (called a "fragment"). M. Conway, *Cat. of Loan Exhibition of Flemish and Belgian Art*, Burlington House, London, 1927, no. 107, pl. L. M. J. Friedländer, IX, 1931, no. 243a. M. Davies, Cat. National Gallery, *Early Netherlandish School*, rev. ed., 1955, p. 120.

Copies of the Entire Composition of a Putative Lost Original:

a. Fig. 75. Zurich, Kunsthaus (Ruzicka-Stiftung). Attributed to the Master of the Half-Lengths (See *infra* Cat. M. H.-L. 9)

b. Fig. 31. Wuppertal-Elberfeld, Von der Heydt Museum (no. 369)

 0.215 x 0.32

 A weak copy, perhaps produced in the Patinir workshop. Munich, Böhler, 1916. *Bibliography*: L. Baldass, 1918, p. 119, n. 2. M. J. Friedländer, IX, 1931, no. 243. *Das von der Heydt-Museum der Stadt Wuppertal*, n.d. (1965), p. 29, illus., p. 33.

c. Fig. 36. Palermo, Prince di Trabia Coll. The composition incorporated in the compositional scheme of the left wing and central panel of a triptych, probably produced in Patinir's studio (see No. 31).

13. LANDSCAPE WITH ECSTASY OF MARY MAGDALENE (Fig. 32)

Zurich, Kunsthaus (No. 24, Ruzicka-Stiftung)

0.26 x 0.36

Comments: I have proposed that this painting is a workshop copy of a lost original by Patinir. It was probably paired with an original composition of the *Landscape with Saint Jerome*, also lost (No. 12 above, and its copies). The two compositions are freely combined in two other paintings which may have originated in Patinir's workshop (No. 31, Fig. 36; and No. 29, Fig. 34).

History: Coll. Achillito Chiesa, Milan (Sale Amer. Art Assoc., New York, I, 27 Nov. 1925, no. 24a, illus.). A. S. Drey, Munich, 1930. Coll. Duensing, Boisenburg. Ruzicka Coll.

Bibliography: M. J. Friedländer, IX, 1931, no. 251, taf. CI (wrongly titled an "Ascension of Mary of Egypt"). G. J. Hoogewerff, 1928, pp. 128-30, fig. 7 (wrongly titled an "Ascension of Mary Magdalene"). Catalogue of the *Gemälde der Ruzicka-Stiftung*, Zurich, Kunsthaus, no. 24, pl. XXVII. R. A. Koch, "La Sainte-Baume in Flemish Landscape Painting of the Sixteenth Century," *G.d.B.-A.*, LXVI, 1965, pp. 273ff., fig. 3.

Copies:

a. Fig. 33. Berlin-Dahlem, Museum. A copy, with stylistic changes, by Herri met de Bles. 0.19 x 0.25

    Bibliography: M. J. Friedländer, XIII, no. 99. R. A. Koch, *loc.cit.*, fig. 7.

b. British Museum. Pen and ink drawing by Jacques de Gheyn the Elder, signed and dated 1600. 0.309 x 0.416. The distant landscape at the right has been changed.

    Bibliography: A. E. Popham, *Cat. of Drawings in the British Museum*, v, London, 1932. Illus. in *Vasari Society*, Part v, 1909-10, no. 19.

14. TRIPTYCH WITH PENITENCE OF ST. JEROME (Frontispiece; Figs. 35, 37-38)

Central Panel: The Penitent St. Jerome

Left Wing: Baptism of Christ (in the distance the Preaching of the Baptist)

Right Wing: St. Anthony Abbot

Exterior: (Grisaille) St. Anne with the Youthful Virgin Mary and Christ Child; St. Sebald

New York, Metropolitan Museum of Art (no. 36.14 A-C)

H. 0.812 x W. 1.203; each wing 0.368 wide. Original frame.

    History: Coll. Emperor Leopold I of Austria (until 1674). Monastery of Kremsmünster, Austria, 1674-1935 (purchased by Knoedler, N.Y.). Acquired by Metropolitan Museum, Fletcher Fund, 1936.

    Bibliography: K. Werner, *Kremsmünster in Wort und Bild*, 1929, p. 54. H. B. Wehle, "A Triptych by Patinir," *Metropolitan Museum Bulletin*, XXXI, 1936, pp. 80-84, illus. p. 81. M. J. Friedländer, XIV, 1937, pp. 118-19, nachtrag taf. XXIX ("a principal work of the Master, the figures are also by his hand"). H. B. Wehle and M. Salinger, *Met. Mus. Cat. of Paintings*, II, *Early Flemish, Dutch & German*, 1947, pp. 115-17.

15. REST ON THE FLIGHT (Fig. 40)

Berlin-Dahlem, Museum (No. 608)

0.62 x 0.78

    History: Coll. Solly, 1821.

    Bibliography: *Königliche Museen zu Berlin, Beschreibendes Verzeichniss der Gemälde*, 1883, no. 608, pp. 334-35. Hulin de Loo, Bruges Exhibition of 1902, *Catalogue critique*, p. 54 (under no. 199). Catalogue of the Kaiser Friedrich Museum, Berlin, II, 1911, p. 138, no. 608. M. Conway, 1921, p. 352. L. Baldass, 1918, p. 119, fig. 4 (Madonna by the workshop of Joos van Cleve). G. J. Hoogewerff, 1928, p. 128, fig. 6. M. J. Friedländer, IX, 1931, no. 237. Exh. Cat. "Paintings from the Berlin Museum," National Gallery, Washington, D.C., 1948, no. 137.

16. REST ON THE FLIGHT (Fig. 39; Figs. 41-43, details)

Madrid, Prado (No. 1611)

1.21 x 1.77

    Bibliography: M. J. Friedländer, 1916, pp. 105-6. L. Baldass, 1918, p. 119. M. Conway, 1921, pp. 350-51. F. Winkler, 1924, p. 216, fig. 131. M. J. Friedländer, IX, 1931, no. 235, pp. 106-8, taf. xcv. G. J. Hoogewerff, 1954, p. 24, pl. 10. *Museo del Prado, Catalogo . . .*, 1952, p. 468, no. 1611 (from the Escorial).

17. TEMPTATION OF ST. ANTHONY (Fig. 44; Figs. 45-47, details)
Madrid, Prado (No. 1615)
1.55 x 1.73   Signed near bottom, right: OPUS JOACHIM *AT*NIER
Comment: A work of collaboration between Patinir and Quentin Massys, attested by an entry in an Escorial inventory of 1574, when Philip II sent the painting there.
Bibliography: Van Mander (Hymans ed.), I, Paris, 1884, p. 196 (notes a signature). C. Justi, "Altflandrische Bilder in Spanien und Portugal, Joachim Patinier und Quentin Metsys," *Z.f.b.K.*, xxi, 1886, pp. 93-95 (discovery of the Escorial inventory). M. J. Friedländer, 1916, p. 184. L. Baldass, 1918, p. 120, fig. 6. M. Conway, 1921, p. 353. M. J. Friedländer, VII, 1929, no. 31, taf. xxx, pp. 45-47. L. Baldass, "Gotik und Renaissance . . . ," Vienna *Jahrbuch*, N.F. VII, 1933, fig. 137 (detail), p. 169. *Museo del Prado, Catalogo . . .* , 1952, p. 469, no. 1615.

18. ST. CHRISTOPHER (Fig. 49; Figs. 50-52, details)
The Escorial (Museum)
1:00 x 1.50 (approximately)
Comment: The figure of St. Christopher is reflected in another composition which may have originated in the Patinir workshop (No. 28, Fig. 53)
Bibliography: M. J. Friedländer, 1916, p. 184. L. Baldass, 1918, p. 119, taf. XII. M. Conway, 1921, pp. 350, 354. E. Panofsky, "Noch Einmal 'Kopie oder Fälschung?,'" *Z.f.b.K.*, LXII, 1928-29, pp. 182-83 (compares the Christopher figure with Dürer's engraving of 1521, B51). M. J. Friedländer, IX, 1931, no. 246, pp. 110-11, taf. C. A. Alvarez Cabanas, "Patinir en el Escorial," *Religión y Cultura*, xxiv, 1933, pp. 362-71. *L'art flamand dans les collections Espagnols*, Bruges, Musée Communal, 1958, no. 43, pp. 77-78.

19. LANDSCAPE WITH CHARON'S BOAT (Fig. 54; Figs. 55-56, details)
Madrid, Prado (No. 1616)
0.64 x 1.03
Bibliography: M. J. Friedländer, 1916, p. 184, taf. 17. L. Baldass, 1918, p. 119. M. Conway, 1921, p. 354. *Museo del Prado, Catalogo . . .* , 1952, p. 469, no. 1616.

II. WORKSHOP

20. REST ON THE FLIGHT (Fig. 19)
Bristol, England, Coll. Mrs. George Kidston
0.313 x 0.560
Comments: Almost certainly a workshop adaptation, made for Lucas Rem, of compositional elements from the Kaufmann-Kaus Triptych (No. 8, Fig. 18) and the Prado *Rest* (No. 16, Fig. 39). In the lower left corner the coat of arms of Rem with his German motto ("ISTZ GVOT SO GEBS GOT"); opposite in the right corner the arms of Rem's wife, Anna Ochainin, with her German motto ("DURCH FIRBE [FÜRBITTE] MARIA U[ND ALLE?] HAILIGEN"). Her

motto is somewhat differently worded in its occurrence on the triptych that Rem commissioned from Massys: "Durch Christ Maria vnd Aler Heilige" (see Chapter 1, notes 38-40). Probably ordered by Rem in Antwerp in 1520.

History: Coll. John Linnell

Bibliography: *Art Treasures of the West Country*, Bristol Museum and Art Gallery, May 25-July 10, 1937, no. 193 (wrongly states that the year "1513" is given in the inscription in Rem's coat of arms. It is the first word "Istz").

21. Landscape with the Rest on the Flight (Fig. 59)
Dijon, Coll. Comte Georges de Vogüé
0.24 x 0.36   Signed near bottom, right of center: Joachim De Patinier
Comments: This very well painted composition is conceivably by Patinir himself. It is an adaptation of the Antwerp *Flight* (No. 2, Fig. 4), with the addition of a fine seaport landscape that also appears in another painting, from the workshop (No. 23, Fig. 57), and in the composition of a follower of Patinir (No. 32, Fig. 58). The grazing ass may have been copied from the Kaufmann-Kaus Triptych (No. 8, Fig. 18). In the distance at the right are the camels and a church in a woods, "borrowed" from the story of Jerome. The figures are not in Patinir's own style, but they are suggestive of that of Joos van Cleve. The Child reaches toward a small bird in flight (cf. No. 26, Fig. 62, where he holds a clumsy bird). The signature in one line is orthographically not in Patinir's manner (see Chapter 1, p. 7, n. 23).

Bibliography: R. Genaille, *De van Eyck à Brueghel*, Paris, 1954, p. 137. J. Lassaigne and L. Delevoy, *La peinture flamande de Jérome Bosch à Rubens*, Geneva, 1958, p. 32. *Les plus belles œuvres des collections de la Côte-d'Or*, Dijon, Musée Municipal, 1958, no. 28, pl. IV.

22. Rest on the Flight (Fig. 61)
Jersey, Channel Islands, Coll. Mrs. Dorothy Hart
1.125 x 1.11
Comments: This painting is a large and handsome adaptation of the landscape style and iconography (in part) of the Master. The picture appears to be the product if not of the workshop then by an imitator in the "circle" of Patinir. The Child reaches forward, while nearby a brown rabbit scratches itself. Not in the style of Patinir himself are the large and small figures, and the types and rendering of the foreground plants.

History: From Palma, Majorca, to England before 1927. Berlin, Trade (L. Blumenreich), 1930. London, Tomas Harris, 1935. Hart Collection since 1936.

Bibliography: M. Conway, *Cat. of Loan Exh. of Flemish and Belgian Art*, Burlington House, London, 1927, No. 121. M. J. Friedländer, IX, 1931, no. 236 ("Madonna figure apparently by another hand"). *L'art flamand dans les collections Britanniques*, Bruges, Musée Communal, 1956, no. 36, pl. 25. *Connoisseur*, 159, no. 641, 1965, fig. 24, p. 154.

23. Rest on the Flight (Fig. 57)
London, National Gallery (No. 3115)
0.33 x 0.459
Comments: This is an "ideal" production of Patinir's workshop since it is a pastiche made

up of elements from three different compositions. The middle distant landscape, with the story of the wheatfield and the pagan temple, is a rearrangement of elements from Patinir's Prado *Rest* (No. 16, Fig. 39). The nursing Madonna, not painted in the style of Patinir, has been adapted from Joos van Cleve's *Rest* (Fig. 14). The distant seaport landscape also appears in another workshop painting (No. 21, Fig. 59), and in a composition by a follower of Patinir (No. 32, Fig. 58).

History: Coll. Sir A. H. Layard (purchased in Madrid in 1871; bequeathed to the National Galley in 1916).

Bibliography: M. Davies, Catalogue National Gallery, *Early Netherlandish School*, rev. ed., 1955, pp. 119-20 ("provisionally ascribed to Patinir's own name").

Copy:

a. Naples, Filangieri Museum (Museo Civico).

0.21 x 0.30 (*Destroyed 30 Sept. 1943*)

Bibliography: G. J. Hoogewerff, 1928, p. 133, fig. 15 ("poor condition"). M. J. Friedländer, IX, 1931, no. 49 (mention as one of several adaptations of the Madonna in Joos van Cleve's *Rest*). M. Davies, *loc.cit.* (Photo Anderson 26324).

24. REST ON THE FLIGHT (Fig. 21)

Minneapolis, Institute of Arts (No. 14.2)

0.35 x 0.50

Comments: The landscape has been copied from the Kaufmann-Kaus Triptych (No. 8, Fig. 18), but the rendering of certain details in the far distance, particularly the trees, lacks the precision of Patinir himself. It is nonetheless an accomplished work, except for the foreground, which appears to have been left unfinished. The figure style of the Madonna, whose robe is a russet hue, is in the manner of Quentin Massys.

History: Coll. Bourgeois, Paris, 1913.

Bibliography: *Bull. Minn. Institute of Arts*, 3, 1914, pp. 130-32. M. J. Friedländer, 1916, p. 184 ("landscape copied from the Kaufmann triptych; changes not in the manner of Patinir"). L. Baldass, 1918, p. 117, n. 1. M. Conway, 1921, p. 353 ("apparently collaboration of Massys and Patinir or a Patinir pupil"). Worcester-Philadelphia Exhibition of Flemish Paintings, 1939, no. 61.

25. REST ON THE FLIGHT (Fig. 60)

Philadelphia, Johnson Collection (No. 377)

0.44 x 0.57

Comments: Despite the high regard in which this painting has been held by Valentiner and van Puyvelde, it is surely no more than a workshop product. Distant landscape at the left and the trees before and behind the Madonna are adapted from the Lugano *Rest* (No. 7, Fig. 12); while the landscape at the right recomposes elements from the Prado *Rest* (No. 16, Fig. 39). The figure of Joseph in the middle distance has also been derived from the latter painting. The high-contrast tonality of the composition is not in the style of Patinir, nor is the figure of the Madonna. She wears a light blue mantle over a dark blue robe.

Bibliography: W. R. Valentiner, *Cat. Johnson Collection*, II, 1913, no. 377, p. 37 ("One

of the finest works of the artist. The figures are by his own hand."). L. Baldass, 1918, p. 114, n. 1 (mentions another variant composition that was in Munich, Trade, Böhler, in 1917, 0.25 x 0.30). M. J. Friedländer, IX, 1931, no. 234. Worcester-Philadelphia Exhibition of Flemish Painting, 1939, no. 60 ("painted about 1521"). L. van Puyvelde, *La peinture flamande au siècle de Bosch et Bruegel*, Paris, 1962, p. 223, figs. 113 and 114 (det.).

26. REST ON THE FLIGHT (Fig. 62)
Stockholm, National Museum (No. 3333)
0.22 x 0.31

Comments: This small painting is another of the many in which the left portion of the landscape was copied from that of the Lugano *Rest* (No. 7, Fig. 12). The painting of the foliage of the trees is not by the hand of Patinir, nor is the figure style of the Madonna, which bears a vague relationship to the style of Joos van Cleve. Perhaps produced in the Patinir shop, though a safer attribution would be "circle" of the Master.

Bibliography: A. Sjöblom, "Kronika aldre Konst. Maleri," *Nationalmusei Arsbok*, Stockholm, IX, 1939, pp. 158-61. *National Museum Stockholm, Foreign Paintings*, 1949, p. 73, w/illus. G. J. Hoogewerff, 1954, pp. 26-27 ("late work, probably by a follower, possibly Joos van Cleve"). A. Bengtsson, "A Painting by Patinir," *Idea and Form*, Uppsala, 1959, p. 93, n. 1 (doubts if by Patinir himself).

27. LANDSCAPE WITH THE BAPTISM OF CHRIST (Fig. 67)
Zurich, Trade (Bührle) (?)
0.33 x 0.455

Comments: The style of the landscape, particularly the cone-like rocks, is removed from that of Patinir; so also is the figure style of the Baptist and Christ, and the group to whom the Baptist preaches in the middle distance. The figures of the Baptism are related to those on the left wing of the Palermo Triptych (No. 31, Fig. 36), a workshop product. This picture might better be called "circle" of the Master. In the lower left hand corner is a faked signature of Patinir.

History: The picture has been in the hands of many dealers: Knoedler, N.Y.; Heinemann, N.Y.; C. Benedict, Paris (1952); Bührle, Zurich, Exh. 1955, (no. 14).

28. ST. CHRISTOPHER (Fig. 53)
0.36 x 0.46
Switzerland, Private Collection (?)

Comments: In a much smaller composition with a completely changed landscape, the figure of Christopher is closely related to that in the Escorial painting (No. 18, Fig. 49). The landscape appears to me to be too weak to justify more than a "workshop" attribution.

Bibliography: M. J. Friedländer, IX, 1931, no. 247 (attributes to Patinir; the picture was then in the Berlin Trade, Haberstock). L. Baldass, "Gotik und Renaissance . . . ," Vienna *Jahrbuch*, N.F. VII, 1933, pp. 155, 157, abb. 127 (accepts as by Patinir). Illustrated in *Atlantis*, XVII, Dec. 1945, p. 546, and color det. on cover.

29. LANDSCAPE WITH ST. JEROME (Fig. 34)

Antwerp, Mayer van den Bergh Museum (No. 367)

0.173 (roundel composition)

Comments: The composition is a free combination of two others by Patinir, on a very small scale (see "Comments" under No. 13). The technique appears to be a little too sketchy for the Master himself, though both style and iconography suggest that it was produced in the workshop.

Bibliography: Catalogue of the Mayer van den Bergh Museum, 1960, no. 367, p. 125 ("atelier" of Patinir). R. A. Koch, "La Sainte-Baume in Flemish Landscape Painting of the Sixteenth Century," *G.d.B.-A.*, LXVI, 1965, pp. 273ff., fig. 6.

30. LANDSCAPE WITH ST. JEROME (Fig. 63)

New York, Trade (formerly Frederick Mont)

0.225 X 0.325

Comments: As discussed in Chapter II, the composition is a reinterpretation of the Louvre painting (No. 10, Fig. 26). This appears to be the original from which the two variant copies listed below were derived. This, as well as the other two, may well have been produced in the workshop of Patinir.

History: The picture has been in the hands of many dealers, as have the presumed copies of it listed below. Perls, Berlin, 1925; Wurzberger, 1948; Frederick Mont, New York.

Copies:

a. Fig. 65. New York and London, Wildenstein & Co.

0.349 x 0.273 (sight)

History: Coll. Dr. Meirowsky, Berlin; earlier in Berlin, Trade (P. Cassirer, 1927).

Bibliography: M. J. Friedländer, IX, 1931, no. 241 (attributed; perhaps a fragment).
A. Marchal in *Le siècle de Bruegel* (Cat. Exh. Brussels Museum), 1963, no. 187, illus. 47.

b. Fig. 64. Present location unknown

0.41 X 0.50

History: Coll. Schoubroeck, Brussels (Sale Brussels, Giroux, 3-5 May 1927, no. 334). Coll. I. Hellberg, Stockholm. Sale Bukowski, Stockholm, Oct. 26-29, 1960, cat. no. 300, illus.

Bibliography: M. J. Friedländer, IX, 1931, no. 241a. G. Lindahl, *Paintings in the Collection of Ivar Hellberg*, Stockholm, 1946, p. 46.

31. TRIPTYCH WITH ST. JEROME (Fig. 36)

Palermo, Prince di Trabia Collection(?)

Central Panel: Jerome Removing Thorn from Lion's Paw

Left Wing: Baptism of Christ and Preaching of John the Baptist

Right Wing: St. Anthony Reading; Rest on the Flight; Ecstasy of Mary Magdalene

Dimensions unknown. Apparently it is about the size of the triptych in the Metropolitan Museum (No. 14).

Comments: The triptych is of special interest because of its relationship to two presumed lost originals by Patinir, as discussed in Chapter II. The design of the figures of the Baptist

and Christ is related to No. 27 (Fig. 67). I was unable to find the collection in Palermo but to judge from the photograph the triptych appears to be no more than a workshop production. It is reproduced, I believe, for the first time, from a photograph in the Gabinetto Fotografico Nazionale, Rome.

Bibliography: G. J. Hoogewerff, 1954, p. 23 ("a complete triptych with very small figures, in which all the favorite motifs of Patinir are brought together, is located, still undescribed, in the collection of the Prince di Trabia in Palermo").

III. ANONYMOUS LATER FOLLOWERS

32. REST ON THE FLIGHT (Fig. 58)
Brussels, Musée de l'Art Ancien (No. 350)
0.245 X 0.350
   Comments: Although the picture is a free combination of elements from other compositions closely related to Patinir (No. 8, Fig. 18, and No. 21, Fig. 59), a circumstance that might qualify this as a workshop product, its impasto technique and atmospheric quality leads me to believe that it was created after the lifetime of Patinir.
   Bibliography: Fierens-Gevaert, *Les primitifs flamands*, Brussels, 1910, III, p. 249, pl. CLXXXX (as Joos van Cleve?). Musées Royaux des B.-A de Belgique, *Catalogue de la peinture ancienne*, 1949, No. 350 (as school of Patinir). G. J. Hoogewerff in *Mededeelingen van het Nederl. Hist. Institut te Rome*, 9, 1939, p. 45, pl. 46, gives it to Mattijs de Cock. The same author in 1954, p. 46, says it is perhaps by Mattijs' pupil W. van Santvoort, who became his pupil in 1540. He wrongly states that a replica of this painting was in the Museum at Namur (Hôtel de Croix). It was the same picture, on loan from the Brussels Museum.

33. LANDSCAPE WITH FLIGHT INTO EGYPT (Fig. 71)
Barcelona, Museo Arte Cataluña (Cambó Bequest, No. 37)
   Comments: This is related to the early *Flight into Egypt* by Patinir—the whole composition vaguely, and the tiny figures of the Holy Family specifically (No. 2, Fig. 4). The graceful figure (a shepherd?) asleep against the tree-stump in the central foreground, the chiaroscuro and restless brushwork are related to the generation which followed Patinir. A composition in the Wetzlar Coll., listed below, appears to be a somewhat simplified variant, though it may well be the original that inspired the painting in Barcelona. Neither, I believe, is from the workshop of Patinir.
   Bibliography: F. J. Sánchez Cantón, *La Colección Cambó*, Barcelona, n.d. (1956), pp. 93-94, no. 37, illus. XLVII.
   Variant:
   a. Amsterdam, Coll. Dr. H. Wetzlar
      0.24 X 0.33
      Comments: See above. Sleeping figure not present; two figures added behind the Holy Family. Formerly in possession of Dr. Heppner, Berlin, and J. Goudstikker, Am-

sterdam. *Bibliography*: *Catalogue of the Wetzlar Coll.*, 1952, no. 74, p. 18, illus. (M. J. Friedländer in Introduction, p. 5, "a thoroughly characteristic work of Patinir, until now unmentioned, as far as I know.") L. van Puyvelde, *La peinture flamande au siècle de Bosch et Bruegel*, Paris, 1962, p. 223 (as Patinir).

34. FLIGHT INTO EGYPT (Fig. 68)
Washington, D.C., National Gallery of Art
0.236 x 0.149

Comments: The little picture was formerly in the collection of the Imperial Gallery in Vienna. There, as early as 1783 it was attributed to Herri met de Bles; later to Patinir; and in 1907 it was attributed by Scheibler to a follower of Patinir, dating ca. 1550. Scheibler noted correctly that the figures are further removed from Patinir's style than the landscape. They are Italianate, somewhat in the style of Correggio.

Bibliography: National Gallery of Art, *Paintings and Sculpture from the Kress Collection, Acquired by the Samuel H. Kress Foundation 1951-1956*, 1956, no. 54, pp. 140-41 (with references to catalogues of the Vienna Gallery).

35. LANDSCAPE WITH TEMPTATION OF CHRIST (Fig. 66)
Banbury, Upton House, Bearsted Coll., National Trust
0.215 x 0.228

Comments: The figure of Christ being tempted by the Devil to turn stones into bread in the foreground suggests a classicizing influence alien to the works of Patinir. The general structure of the landscape, though patterned after the Master, is weak. The third phase of the Temptation of Christ may be seen on the distant rocky mountain. Two figures with a camel are in the middle distance.

History: Sale of the Rosenthal Coll., Sotheby, London, 21 Apr. 1937. Viscount Bearsted Coll., Upton House.

Bibliography: *Catalogue of the Bearsted Collection*, 1950, no. 162. Exhibited Whitechapel Art Gallery, 1955, cat. no. 86, illus. *Upton House, the Bearsted Collection: Pictures*, The National Trust, 1964, no. 162, pl. VI b.

36. LANDSCAPE WITH SHEPHERDS (Fig. 69)
Schoten (Antwerp), Coll. Michel de Pret-Roose de Calesberg
0.45 x 0.375   Signed on tree-trunk, lower right: OPUS/JOACHIM/D PATINIR

Comments: First published by G. Marlier in 1954 and accepted by every critic since (see below). Although "properly signed" and possessing certain features of Patinir's early style as they may be observed in the Karlsruhe *Jerome*, for example (No. 1), the picture has for me a certain hard and dry quality that points to the generation that follows Patinir and a style not dissimilar to that of the Master of the Half-Lengths. Compositionally, the delimitation of space on either side by trees that are cut by the picture frame is a sophistication that one does not expect of Patinir.

The owner of the picture has kindly informed me that an X-ray examination of the painting by the A.C.L. in Brussels revealed three compositional changes: "The swans were

considerably larger and 'in' the water instead of 'on' it; the headdress of a shepherd has been altered; and the first walking figure [of the procession in the middle distance] held a sword and a flag instead of a stick."

The subject is puzzling, for this is more than a simple pastoral scene. Evidently shepherds have witnessed a miracle, indicated by its golden rays, within a wayside shrine, while a procession on horseback and on foot approaches from the background. Perhaps the scene illustrates some local legend.

Bibliography: G. Marlier, *Erasme et la peinture flamande de son temps*, Damme, 1954, pp. 161, 167 n. 26, fig. 15 (by Patinir). J. Lassaigne & R. Delevoy, *La peinture flamande de Jérome Bosch à Rubens*, Geneva, 1958, p. 32 (early work of Patinir; "archaizing, continuing the tradition of the miniaturists"). E. Gérard, *Dinant et la Meuse dans l'histoire du paysage*, Lammersdorf, 1960, p. 95. L. van Puyvelde, *La peinture flamande au siècle de Bosch et Breughel*, Brussels and Paris (Elsevier/Meddens), 1962, p. 222 (by Patinir). A. Marchal in *Le siècle de Bruegel* (Cat. Exh. Brussels Museum), 1963, no. 196, illus. 56 ("youthful work of Patinir").

IV. LANDSCAPES BY THE MASTER OF THE HALF-LENGTHS

M. H.-L. 1. Landscape with Flight into Egypt (Fig. 81; Fig. 82, detail)
Raleigh, The North Carolina Museum of Art (No. 126)
0.65 x 0.63

Comments: A mature masterpiece, entirely by the hand of the Master of the Half-Lengths. The unusual, nearly square shape of the panel is the same size as the Master's *Rest on the Flight* in Copenhagen (Fig. 87). They are not a pair, as Hoogewerff points out (see below), because of differing scale relationships of figures to landscape. Mary and Joseph wear bright red mantels.

A large variant composition of the figure group with a landscape background (0.55 x 0.43) was in the Ittersum Coll., sold by F. Muller, Amsterdam, 14 May 1912, no. 160 (as "School of Patinir"); recently in New York, Trade (Koetser), 1952.

History: Coll. Marquess Gentile, Genoa.

Bibliography: A. Morassi, *Capolavori della pittura a Genova*, 1951, pp. 75, 102, figs. 173-75 (attributed to Patinir and the Master of the Half-Lengths). G. J. Hoogewerff, 1954, p. 25, fig. 13 (landscape by Patinir). North Carolina Museum of Art, *Cat. of Paintings*, Raleigh, 1956, no. 126, p. 64 (Patinir and the Master of the Half-Lengths). C. W. Stanford, Jr., *Masterpieces in the North Carolina Museum of Art*, Raleigh, 1966, pp. 38-41 (Patinir and the Master of the Half-Lengths).

M. H.-L. 2. Rest on the Flight (Fig. 91)
Basel, Öffentliche Kunstsammlung (No. 1355)
0.375 x 0.51

Comments: Labeled by the Basel Museum as "Circle of Patinir," the figure style is not

quite that of the Master of the Half-Lengths himself, though modeled upon it; and the landscape is not as sharply delineated as in his best works, though many features of his landscape iconography are present. Probably workshop.

History: Prof. J. J. Bachofen-Burckhardt-Stiftung, 1920.

Bibliography: Öffentliche Kunstsammlung, Basel, *Katalog*, i, 1957, p. 118.

M. H.-L. 3.   Rest on the Flight (Fig. 87)
Copenhagen, National Museum of Art (No. 1743)
0.65 x 0.64

Comments: One of the much discussed paintings by the Master, formerly thought by Friedländer (and many others) to have been painted in collaboration with Patinir. A mature work entirely by the hand of the Master of the Half-Lengths.

History: Purchased in Florence in 1902.

Bibliography: K. Madsen, *Catalogue of the Copenhagen Gallery*, 1904, p. 103, no. 238b ("landscape by Patinir, figures in style of Master of the Half-Lengths"). M. J. Friedländer, 1916, p. 108 (cites and agrees with Madsen). L. Baldass, 1918, p. 126 ("entirely by the Master of the Half-Lengths"). W. Burger, *Die Malerei in den Niederlanden* 1400-1550, 1925, p. 119, taf. 178 ("collaboration"). M. J. Friedländer, ix, 1931, p. 121 (no longer believes in Patinir's participation). M. J. Friedländer, xii, 1935, nos. 71 and 75 (the same picture catalogued twice in error; "the landscape under the influence of Patinir"). G. J. Hoogewerff, 1954, p. 25 ("collaboration").

M. H.-L. 4.   Rest on the Flight (Fig. 89)
New York, New York Historical Society
0.663 x 0.938

Comments: The landscape is completely in conformity with the style and iconography of the Master of the Half-Lengths, but oddly enough the figure style is that of a different painter, perhaps the Master of 1518.

History: Coll. Quedeville. Coll. Thomas J. Bryan, N.Y., 1867 ("School of Dürer").

Bibliography: F. J. Mather, Jr., "An Unpublished Patinir," *Burlington Mag.*, vii, 1905, p. 480 (cites an earlier attribution to Patinir by W. Bode in *Z.f.b.K.*, 1895, pp. 13ff.). M. J. Friedländer, xii, 1935, no. 76 (as by the Master of the Half-Lengths).

M. H.-L. 5.   Landscape with Rest on the Flight (Fig. 79; Fig. 80, detail)
Vienna, Kunsthistorisches Museum (No. 950)
0.385 x 0.515

Comments: In the earlier catalogues of the Vienna Museum the painting was variously attributed to either Patinir or Herri met de Bles. First recognized by Baldass, quite correctly I believe, as by the Master of the Half-Lengths. Probably an early work.

Bibliography: L. Baldass, 1918, p. 126, taf. xiii. F. Winkler, 1924, p. 383 ("the figures but not the landscape by the Master"). M. J. Friedländer, xii, 1935, no. 77 (by the Master though "the rich Landscape, in Patinir's manner, perhaps by another hand"). O. Benesch, "The Name

of the Master of the Half-Lengths," *G.d.B.-A.*, LXXXV, 1943, p. 272 and fig. 7 (as Hans Vereycke). *Cat. of the Kunsthistorisches Museum, Gemäldegalerie*, II, 1958, no. 394 (as Hans Vereycke).

M. H.-L. 6. Landscape with Scenes of John the Baptist (Fig. 83)

Uppsala, University Museum (Nos. 322-323)

0.31 x 0.70

Comments: This unusually broad panel had at some unknown date been sawed into two independent pictures, nearly square in shape (an interesting commentary on its composition!). Cleaned in 1953, it was discovered that the two parts belonged together, and they have been reunited. Friedländer had attributed them to Patinir, and the attribution has remained to date. The picture is, I believe, a very characteristic and mature work by the Master of the Half-Lengths.

Bibliography: M. J. Friedländer, IX, 1931, nos. 222 and 223 (as Patinir). A. Bengtsson, "A Painting by Joachim Patinir," *Idea and Form*, Stockholm, 1959, pp. 88-94, with illustrations ("to be dated after 1520").

M. H.-L. 7. Landscape with John the Baptist Preaching (Fig. 86)

Montreal, L. V. Randall Coll.

0.18 x 0.23 (narrow strip of wood added to top of panel)

Comments: A hitherto unpublished painting of fine quality that I feel to be a characteristic work in the mature style of the Master of the Half-Lengths. Its owner, Prof. Randall, made the following perceptive observation in a letter to me: "The landscape is very beautiful; the figures are better than in almost any Patinir painting I know. There is however something in the style of the painting which might suggest a very slightly later date (5 to 10 years)." The picture should be compared with the painting in Uppsala, Fig. 83. A similar compositional treatment of the same theme occurs in a painting attributed (by Georges Marlier) to Cornelis Massys, now in the Wetzlar Coll. in Amsterdam (exhibited in *Le siècle de Bruegel*, Brussels Museum, 1963, no. 155, illus. 110).

M. H.-L. 8. Landscape with St. Jerome (Fig. 77; Fig. 78, detail)

Kansas City, W. R. Nelson Gallery of Art (No. 61-1)

0.355 x 0.49

Comments: First published by G. J. Hoogewerff in 1926 as an important work of Patinir (and accepted by Friedländer on the basis of the reproduction in Hoogewerff's article), the painting is, I believe, one of the most significant landscapes of the Master of the Half-Lengths. It is an early work and must have been painted shortly after the *Landscape with St. Jerome* in Zurich (M. H.-L. 9, Fig. 75). The little figures are quite in the style of the Master, and that of Jerome is very similar to a later representation by the Master of the penitent Saint in an upright format (present location unknown; once in Vienna, Galerie Sankt Lucas, cat. no. 52, date?, illustrated). Characteristic landscape features in this painting, as discussed in Chapter IV, include the flights of birds in the sky, the rock mass on the distant horizon which

projects at an angle, the low-arched bridge in the foreground, and the treatment of the grasses and ferns in the foreground.

History: Coll. Mengarini, Rome. Coll. Castellino, Rome.

Bibliography: G. J. Hoogewerff, 1926, abb. 9; 1928, p. 131 and fig. 10; 1954, p. 23, fig. 11. M. J. Friedländer, IX, 1931, no. 244. *Nelson Gallery Bulletin*, III, 3, 1961, illus. p. 14.

M. H.-L. 9.   LANDSCAPE WITH ST. JEROME (Fig. 75; Fig. 76, detail)

Zurich, Kunsthaus (No. 23, Ruzicka-Stiftung)

0.255 X 0.35

Comments: Hitherto published as a work by Patinir, the picture is discussed in Chapter IV as the hypothetically earliest known landscape painting by the Master of the Half-Lengths. It copies a lost original, I believe, by Patinir that has survived in several examples, including a copy by Patinir himself of the left half of the composition (No. 12, Fig. 30). The lost original was probably paired with a *Landscape with the Ecstasy of Mary Magdalene* of which a Patinir workshop copy survives in Zurich together with this picture (No. 13, Fig. 32).

The style of the small figures, including the seated Jerome, is that of the Master of the Half-Lengths. The pair of turbaned figures in the left foreground is a favorite creation that appears in several other compositions, while the motif of the woodchoppers is adapted in M. H.-L. 8, Fig. 78, detail. Characteristically, the Master fills the landscape with human activity and with animals, including leaping rabbits and a magpie. The stylized treatment of the foreground vegetation also keynotes his style.

History: Coll. Achillito Chiesa, Milan (Sale Amer. Art Assoc., New York, I, 27 Nov. 1925, no. 24, illus.). A. S. Drey, Munich, 1930. Coll. Duensing, Boisenburg. Ruzicka Coll.

Bibliography: M. J. Friedländer, IX, 1931, no. 243b, taf. XCVIII. G. J. Hoogewerff, 1928, p. 130, fig. 8. Catalogue of the *Gemälde der Ruzicka-Stiftung*, Zurich, Kunsthaus, no. 23, pl. XXVI. M. Davies, Cat. National Gallery, *Early Netherlandish School*, rev. ed., 1955, p. 120.

M. H.-L. 10.   ST. JOHN ON PATMOS (Fig. 88, detail, upper half)

London, National Gallery (No. 717)

0.36 X 0.24

Comments: Both figure and landscape style are completely characteristic of the Master. The surface of the painting has been somewhat abraded.

Bibliography: M. J. Friedländer, 1916, p. 108 ("perhaps in collaboration with Patinir"). L. Baldass, 1918, p. 126 ("entirely by the Master of the Half-Lengths"). M. J. Friedländer, IX, 1931, p. 121 (no longer believes in collaboration). M. J. Friedländer, XII, 1935, no. 80. M. Davies, Cat. National Gallery, *Early Netherlandish School*, rev. ed., 1955, p. 88, no. 717 (cautiously labels "Studio").

M. H.-L. 11.   LANDSCAPE WITH PENITENT MAGDALENE (Fig. 84)

Dijon, Musée municipal (No. D. 212)

0.67 X 1.07

Comments: The figure style is that of the Master (cf. Friedländer, XII, taf. XII), and the restlessness of the landscape would appear to warrant a relatively early date in his career. The

background teems with animals and figures; many of the latter are pilgrims going to and from the mountainous site of La Sainte-Baume, though the actual site is not copied from Patinir's picture (cf. Cat. 1, No. 13, Fig. 32).

Bibliography: J. Marette, *Connaissance des Primitifs par l'étude du bois*, Paris, 1961, p. 179, no. 122, pl. XXXIII (called "Patinir").

M. H.-L. 12. LANDSCAPE WITH LUCRETIA(?) (Fig. 90)

Brussels, Trade (Willems), 1957

0.23 X 0.275

Comments: This unpublished picture, somewhat rubbed, contains many features characteristic of the Master in addition to the figure style, notably the low-arched bridge, type of distant mountain, fountain with Cupid, and foreground vegetation. Lucretia(?), about to plunge a sword into her breast, recalls a similar motif in prints by Marcantonio Raimondi. An odd subject for a landscape painting, Lucretia was depicted by Jan Gossart, Joos van Cleve, and many other Flemish masters of the time. The horse appears to have been added later, perhaps in the early 17th century (Ch. de Tolnay, verbally). Perhaps a workshop product.

M. H.-L. 13. LANDSCAPE WITH HUNTING PARTY (Fig. 85)

Present location unknown (formerly Berlin, Wesendonk Coll.)

0.445 X 0.555

Comments: The picture has been deemed to be a characteristic work by Patinir though Baldass long ago attributed it, correctly I think, to the Master of the Half-Lengths. It is a completely typical work of his mature style.

History: Berlin, Wesendonk Coll. (acquired in Rome in 1860). On loan to Kaiser Friedrich Museum, Berlin, 1917. Anonymous loan to Birmingham, England, City Museum, 1962.

Bibliography: *Cat. Wesendonk Coll.*, Berlin, 1880, no. 230 (Patinir). H. Hymans, *L'exposition des primitifs flamands à Bruges*, Paris, 1902, reprod. p. 67 (Patinir). L. Baldass, 1918, p. 126 and n. 2, figs. 11, 12 (Master of the Half-Lengths). F. Winkler, 1924, p. 383 (Master of the Half-Lengths). E. Heidrich, *Alt-Niederländische Malerei*, Jena, 1924, p. 46, abb. 121 (late work by Patinir). M. J. Friedländer, IX, 1931, no. 256 (Patinir). A. Lhote, *Treatise on Landscape Painting* (tr. W. J. Strachan), London, 1950, pl. 23 (Patinir).

BIBLIOGRAPHY

SELECTED WORKS ON PATINIR

Baldass, L., "Die niederländische Landschaftsmalerei von Patinir bis Bruegel," Vienna *Jahrbuch* (*Jahrbuch der Kunsthistorischen Sammlungen, Wien*), xxxiv, 1918, pp. 111ff.

——, "Ein Landschaftsbild von Matthys Cock," *Zeitschrift für bildende Kunst*, 61, 1927, pp. 90-96.

——, "Joachim Patiniers Christophorus-Zeichnung," *Mitt. der gesell. für vervielfältigende Kunst* (*Beilage der Graphischen Künste*), 51, 1928, pp. 23-24.

——, "Gotik und Renaissance im Werke des Quinten Metsys," Vienna *Jahrbuch*, N.F. VII, 1933, pp. 153-73.

Benesch, O., "Meisterzeichnungen des 15. und 16. Jahrhunderts aus dem Südniederländischen Kunstkreis," *Annuaire des Musées royaux des Beaux-Arts de Belgique*, I, 1938, pp. 34-37.

——, "The Name of the Master of the Half-Lengths," *Gazette des Beaux-Arts*, LXXXV, 1943, pp. 269-82.

Bengtsson, A., "A Painting by Patinir," *Idea and Form*, Figura Nova Series 1, Uppsala, 1959, pp. 88-94.

Białostocki, J., "Nouvelles notes sur L'Album Errera," *Bulletin des Musées royaux des Beaux-Arts de Belgique*, 1955, pp. 233-38.

Conway, M., *The Van Eycks and their Followers*, New York, 1921, pp. 348ff.

Davies, M., *Early Netherlandish School* (Catalogue of the National Gallery, London), rev. ed., 1955, pp. 119-21.

Fierens-Gevaert, *Les Primitifs Flamands*, III, Brussels, 1910, pp. 217-20.

Friedländer, M. J., *Meisterwerke . . . der Austellung zu Brügge*, 1902, Munich, 1903.

——, *Von Eyck bis Bruegel*, Berlin, 1916 (1st ed.); 1921 (2d ed.). English translation, with annotations, *From van Eyck to Bruegel*, New York (Phaidon Press), 1956, pp. 76ff.

——, *Die altniederländische Malerei*, IX (Patinir), 1931, pp. 101-24; addenda in Vol. XIV, 1937, pp. 118-19; Vol. XII (Master of the Half-Lengths), 1935, pp. 25-32.

——, *Essays über die Landschaftsmalerei*, The Hague, 1947, pp. 54-67.

Gérard, E., *Dinant et la Meuse dans l'histoire du paysage*, Lammersdorf, 1960.

Goffin, A., "Flandre et Italie," *Revue d'art* (Antwerp), XL, 1922.

Helbig, J., "Joachim Patenier," *Revue de l'art chrétien*, 4th ser., XI, 1900, pp. 463-71.

——, in *Biographie Nationale de Belgique*, 16, 1901, pp. 679-89.

——, *L'Art mosan*, I, 1906, pp. 138ff.

Hoogewerff, G. J., *Nederlandsche Schilders in Italië in de XVIe Eeuw*, Utrecht, 1912, pp. 228-32.

——, "Joachim Patenier in Italië," *Onze Kunst*, 43, 1926, pp. 1-26.

——, "Joachim Patenier en Italie," *Revue d'art* (Antwerp), XLV, 1928, pp. 117-34. (Tr. and emendation of the preceding article.)

——, *Het Landschap van Bosch tot Rubens*, Antwerp, 1954, pp. 17-27.

Hulin de Loo, G., *Catalogue critique*, Bruges Exhibition of 1902, Ghent, 1902, p. 54.

Hymans, H., ed. of *Van Mander, Le Livre de peintres*, I, Paris, 1884, pp. 192-96.

Justi, C., "Altflandrische Bilder in Spanien und Portugal, Joachim Patinier und Quentin Metsys," *Zeitschrift für bildenden Kunst*, xxi, 1886, pp. 93-95.

Koch, R., "La Sainte-Baume in Flemish Landscape Painting of the Sixteenth Century," *Gazette des Beaux-Arts*, lxvi, 1965, pp. 273-82.

Krönig, W., *Der italienische Einfluss in der flämischen Malerei im ersten Drittel des 16. Jahrhunderts*, Würzburg, 1936.

Lampsonius, D., ed. and tr. by J. Puraye, *Dominique Lampson, Les Effigies des peintres célèbres des Pays-Bas*, Bruges (Desclée de Brouwer), 1956, pp. 38-39.

Lassaigne, J. and R. Delevoy, *La peinture flamande de Jérôme Bosch à Rubens*, Geneva, 1958, pp. 29-33.

Lhote, A., *Treatise on Landscape Painting*, tr. W. J. Strachan, London, 1950.

Löhneysen, H.-W. von, *Künstler und Kritiker*, Eisenach, 1956, pp. 388-92.

Mander, K. van, *Het Schilderboek*, Haerlem, 1604 (1st ed.), fol. 219r.

Marchal, A., in *Le siècle de Bruegel* (Catalogue of Exhibition, Musées royaux des Beaux-Arts de Belgique, Brussels), 1963, pp. 144-48.

Marlier, G., *Erasme et la peinture flamande de son temps*, Damme, 1954.

Michel, E., Le Louvre, *Catalogue Raisonné . . . Peintures Flamandes du XVe et du XVIe Siècles*, Paris, 1953, pp. 236-38.

Michiels, A., *Histoire de la peinture flamande*, iv, 2d ed., Paris, 1866.

Nagler, G., *Künstler-Lexicon*, xi, 1841, pp. 12-14.

Pinchart, A. and C. Ruelens, "Les historiens de la peinture flamande," Notes included in Crowe and Cavalcaselle, *Anciens peintres flamands*, i, Brussels, 1862, pp. cclxxx-vi.

Piron, A., "Nouvelles recherches concernant les peintres Joachim le Patinier et Henri Bles," *La Nouvelle Revue Wallonne*, xiv, 1965, pp. 101-12, 157-71, 215-45; xv, 1965, pp. 41-47.

Puyvelde, L. van, *La peinture flamande au siècle de Bosch et Breughel*, Brussels and Paris (Elsevier/Meddens), 1962, pp. 221-23.

Rombouts, P. and T. van Lerius, *Les Liggeren*, i, Antwerp, 1872, p. 83.

Rooses, M., *Geschichte der Malerschule Antwerpens*, Munich, 1889, pp. 115-16.

Sandrart, J., *Der Teutschen Academie (zweyter Theil)*, Nuremberg, 1675, p. 244.

Sjöblom, A., "Kronika aldre Konst. Maleri," *Nationalmusei Arsbok*, Stockholm, ns ix, 1939, pp. 158-61.

Thiéry, Y., *Le paysage flamand au xvii siècle*, Paris, 1953, introductory chapter.

Vaudoyer, J.-L., "Joachim Patenier," *L'Art et les Artistes*, ns vi, 1922-23, pp. 85-92.

Veth, J. and S. Muller, *Albrecht Dürers niederländische Reise*, ii, Berlin, 1918, pp. 211ff.

Vollmer, H., in *Thieme-Becker*, xxvi, 1932, pp. 292-93.

Wauters, A., *The Flemish School of Painting*, London, 1885.

Wehle, H., "A Triptych by Patinir," *Bulletin of the Metropolitan Museum of Art*, 31, 1936, pp. 80-84.

BIBLIOGRAPHY

Wetering, C. van de, *Die Entwicklung der niederländische Landschaftsmalerei vom Anfang des 16. Jahrhunderts bis zur Jahrhundertmitte*, Berlin, 1938, pp. 24-30.

Willis, F., "Zur Kenntnis der Antwerpener Kleinmeister des frühen 16. Jahrhunderts," *Monatshefte für Kunstwissenschaft*, VII, 1914, pp. 43-47.

Winkler, F., *Die altniederländische Malerei*, Berlin, 1924.

Wurzbach, A. von, *Niederländisches Künstlerlexicon*, II, Vienna, 1910, pp. 308-11; III, 1911, p. 131.

INDEX

95

1. Patinir, *Landscape with St. Jerome*. Karlsruhe, Kunsthalle (Cat. No. 1)

2. Patinir, *Landscape with Burning of Sodom*. Rotterdam, Boymans-Van Beuningen Museum (Cat. No. 3)

3. Patinir, Workshop, *Landscape with Burning of Sodom*. Oxford, Ashmolean Museum (Cat. No. 3a)

4. Patinir, *Landscape with Flight into Egypt*. Antwerp, Museum (Cat. No. 2)

5. Detail of Fig. 4

6. Patinir, *Landscape with Martyrdom of St. Catherine*. Vienna, Kunsthistorisches Museum (Cat. No. 4)

7. Detail of Fig. 6

8. Patinir, *Baptism of Christ*. Vienna, Kunsthistorisches Museum (Cat. No. 5)

9. Detail of Fig. 8

10. Patinir, *Landscape with Preaching of John the Baptist*. Brussels, Museum (Cat. No. 6)

11. Patinir, Workshop, *Landscape with Preaching of John the Baptist*. Philadelphia,
Museum of Art (Cat. No. 6a)

12. Patinir, *Landscape with Rest on the Flight*. Lugano, Thyssen Coll. (Cat. No. 7)

13. Patinir, Workshop, *Landscape with Grazing Ass*. Rotterdam,
Boymans-Van Beuningen Museum (Cat. No. 7a)

14. Joos van Cleve, *Rest on the Flight*. Brussels, Museum

15. Detail of Fig. 14

16. Detail of Fig. 18: Central panel

17. Detail of Fig. 18: Flanking panels

18. Patinir, *Triptych with Rest on the Flight*. Frankfurt, W. Kaus Coll. Formerly Berlin, Kaufmann Coll. (Cat. No. 8)

19. Patinir, Workshop, *Rest on the Flight*. Bristol, Mrs. G. Kidston Coll. (Cat. No. 20)

20. Patinir, *Assumption of the Virgin*. Philadelphia, John G. Johnson Coll. (Cat. No. 9)

21. Patinir, Workshop, *Rest on the Flight*. Minneapolis, Institute of Arts (Cat. No. 24)

22. Detail of Fig. 20

23. Detail of Fig. 20

24. Detail of Fig. 20

25. Detail of Fig. 20

26. Patinir, *Landscape with St. Jerome*. Paris, Louvre (Cat. No. 10)

27. Patinir, Workshop, *Landscape with St. Jerome*. Venice, Ca d'Oro (Cat. No. 10a)

28. Patinir, *Landscape with St. Jerome*. Madrid, Prado (Cat. No. 11)

29. Detail of Fig. 28

30. Patinir, *Landscape with St. Jerome*. London, National Gallery (Cat. No. 12)

31. Patinir, Workshop, *Landscape with St. Jerome*. Wuppertal-
Elberfeld, Von der Heydt Museum (Cat. No. 12b)

32. Patinir, Workshop, *Landscape with Ecstasy of Mary Magdalene*. Zurich, Kunsthaus (Cat. No. 13)

33. Herri met de Bles, *Mountain Landscape*. Berlin-Dahlem, Museum (Cat. No. 13a)

34. Patinir, Workshop, *Landscape with St. Jerome*. Antwerp,
Van den Bergh Museum (Cat. No. 29)

35. Patinir, *Triptych with Penitence of St. Jerome.* New York, Metropolitan Museum (Cat. No. 14)

36. Patinir, Workshop, *Triptych with St. Jerome.* Palermo, di Trabia Coll. (Cat. No. 31)

37. Detail of Fig. 35

38. Patinir, *Triptych with St. Jerome, Exterior*. New York, Metropolitan Museum (Cat. No. 14)

39. Patinir, *Rest on the Flight*. Madrid, Prado (Cat. No. 16)

40. Patinir, *Rest on the Flight*. Berlin-Dahlem, Museum (Cat. No. 15)

41. Detail of Fig. 39

42. Detail of Fig. 39

43. Detail of Fig. 39

44. Patinir and Quentin Massys, *Temptation of St. Anthony*. Madrid, Prado (Cat. No. 17)

45. Detail of Fig. 44

46. Detail of Fig. 44

47. Detail of Fig. 44

48. Jan Wellens de Cock, *Temptation of St. Anthony*. Woodcut, 1522

49. Patinir, *St. Christopher*. Escorial (Cat. No. 18)

50. Detail of Fig. 49

51. Detail of Fig. 49

52. Detail of Fig. 49

53. Patinir, Workshop, *St. Christopher*. Switzerland, Private Coll. (Cat. No. 28)

54. Patinir, *Landscape with Charon's Boat*. Madrid, Prado (Cat. No. 19)

55. Detail of Fig. 54

56. Detail of Fig. 54

57. Patinir, Workshop, *Rest on the Flight*. London, National Gallery (Cat. No. 23)

58. Follower of Patinir, *Landscape with Rest on the Flight*. Brussels, Museum (Cat. No. 32)

59. Patinir, Workshop, *Landscape with Rest on the Flight*. Dijon, de Vogüé Coll. (Cat. No. 21)

60. Patinir, Workshop, *Rest on the Flight*. Philadelphia, John G. Johnson Coll. (Cat. No. 25)

61. Circle of Patinir, *Rest on the Flight*. Jersey, Channel Islands, Mrs. Dorothy Hart Coll. (Cat. No. 22)

62. Circle of Patinir, *Rest on the Flight*. Stockholm, National Museum (Cat. No. 26)

63. Patinir, Workshop, *Landscape with St. Jerome*. New York. Frederick Mont, formerly (Cat. No. 30)

64. Patinir, Workshop, *Landscape with St. Jerome*, Stockholm, Hellberg Coll., formerly (Cat. No. 30b)

65. Patinir, Workshop, *Landscape with St. Jerome*. New York, Wildenstein (Cat. No. 30a)

66. Follower of Patinir, *Landscape with Temptation of Christ*. Banbury, Upton House,
Bearsted Coll., National Trust (Cat. No. 35)

67. Circle of Patinir, *Landscape with Baptism of Christ*
Zurich, Bührle (?) (Cat. No. 27)

68. Follower of Patinir, *Flight into Egypt*. Washington, National Gallery (Cat. No. 34)

69. Follower of Patinir, *Landscape with Shepherds*. Schoten-Antwerp, de Pret-Roose Coll. (Cat. No. 36)

70. Joos van Cleve (attributed to), *Virgin and Child with Dominican*. Paris, Louvre

71. Follower of Patinir, *Landscape with Flight into Egypt*.
Barcelona, Museo Arte Cataluña (Cat. No. 33)

72. Joos van Cleve, Workshop, *Rest on the Flight*. Munich, Pinakothek

73. Master of the Half-Lengths, *Rest on the Flight*. London, National Gallery

74. Master of the Half-Lengths, *Rest on the Flight*. Philadelphia, John G. Johnson Coll.

75. Master of the Half-Lengths, *Landscape with St. Jerome*. Zurich, Kunsthaus (Cat. No. M. H.-L. 9)

76. Detail of Fig. 75

77. Master of the Half-Lengths, *Landscape with St. Jerome*. Kansas City,
Nelson Gallery (Cat. No. M. H.-L. 8)

78. Detail of Fig. 77

79. Master of the Half-Lengths, *Landscape with Rest on the Flight*. Vienna, Kunsthistorisches Museum (Cat. M. H.-L. 5)

80. Detail of Fig. 79

81. Master of the Half-Lengths, *Landscape with Flight into Egypt*. Raleigh, North Carolina
Museum of Art (Cat. No. M. H-L. 1)

82. Detail of Fig. 81

83. Master of the Half-Lengths, *Landscape with Scenes of John the Baptist.* Uppsala,
University Museum (Cat. No. M. H.-L. 6)

84. Master of the Half-Lengths, *Landscape with Penitent Magdalene.* Dijon, Museum (Cat. No. M. H.-L. 11)

85. Master of the Half-Lengths, *Landscape with Hunting Party.* Formerly Berlin, Wesendonk Coll. (Cat. No. M. H.-L. 13)

86. Master of the Half-Lengths, *Landscape with Preaching of John the Baptist.*
Montreal, L. V. Randall Coll. (Cat. No. M. H.-L. 7)

87. Master of the Half-Lengths, *Rest on the Flight*. Copenhagen, Museum (Cat. No. M. H.-L. 3)

88. Master of the Half-Lengths, *St. John on Patmos* (detail). London,
National Gallery (Cat. M. H.-L. 10)

89. Master of the Half-Lengths and Master of 1518 (?), *Rest on the Flight*.
New York, N.Y. Historical Society (Cat. M. H.-L. 4)

90. Master of the Half-Lengths, Workshop, *Landscape with Lucretia* (?).
Brussels, Willems (Cat. M. H.-L. 12)

91. Master of the Half-Lengths, Workshop, *Rest on the Flight*. Basel,
Öffentliche Kunstsammlung (Cat. M. H.-L. 2)

92. Adriaen Isenbrandt, *Landscape with St. Hubert*.
Berlin-Dahlem, Museum